Minorities, Schools, and Politics

Canadian Historical Readings

A selection of articles from the *Canadian Historical Review* and other volumes

Edited by Ramsay Cook / Craig Brown / Carl Berger

Minorities, Schools, and Politics

Essays by D. G. Creighton/W. L. Morton
Ramsay Cook/Manoly R. Lupul/Marilyn Barber
Margaret Prang

Introduction by Craig Brown

University of Toronto Press

© University of Toronto Press 1969
Printed in Canada
SBN 8020 1617 0

Contents

Introduction

CRAIG BROWN

THE ESSAYS IN THIS VOLUME have been selected to illustrate a portion of the most difficult and complex continuous problem in Canadian history, the relationship between the French-speaking minority and the English-speaking majority. The point at issue is the kind of education afforded to the children of the minority in the provinces of Manitoba and Ontario and in the North-West Territories. That that was the most critical and most explosive issue in French-English relations between 1880 and 1920 is beyond doubt. Both the French-speaking and the English-speaking Canadians involved in these disputes clearly recognized that the continuing viability of the French Canadian's identity outside the province of Quebec was dependent upon the mode and content of instruction given to French-speaking pupils. Both asserted that if that mode and content of instruction were wholly English in character, the "French fact" in Ontario, Manitoba, and in the Territories soon to become Saskatchewan and Alberta would gradually wither away. Their point of difference was whether that could or should be allowed to happen.

No attempt has been made by the editors to present all of the relevant material on these minority schools' crises. The second volume of the *Report of the Royal Commission on Bilingualism and Biculturalism* points out that over the years of these crises the basic issue in question shifted from religion and denominational schools to the use of the French language in the instruction of children of the minority. Throughout these disputes the problems of religion and language were mixed together, adding to the confusion and the complexity of the disputes. But the language issue was undoubtedly the more important to the minority in the long run and these essays are primarily concerned with that problem. Professors Morton and Cook are concerned with the resolution of the Manitoba schools question after the denominational issue had been "settled" in the decisions of the Judicial Committee of the Privy Council in 1892 and 1895 and the Laurier-Greenway Agreement of 1897. Professor Lupul devotes his attention to the Roman Catholic hierarchy's attempts to secure a French-language school inspector for the denominational schools in the Territories in a period when the Church's control over its schools was being progressively taken over by the territorial government. And Professors Barber and Prang sketch out the controversy in Ontario over bilingual schools which turned English-speaking and French-speaking proponents of separate schools against each other.

Four common themes run through these essays. The first is that all of them note a basic causal relationship between demographic change and the crises over minority schools. In Manitoba and in the Territories the school systems were established in 1870 and 1875, in both cases at a very early stage in the development of the community. The denominational schools systems reflected the tentative equality of French and English social and political forces in these undeveloped communities at the time. But by the last decade of the nineteenth century both communities were experiencing growing population and social change caused by the influx of great numbers of English-speaking immigrants. The new settlers found the institutions of the community inadequate for their needs and used their political power to change those institutions: in Manitoba to abolish separate (French) schools and adopt a "national " (public and English) school system; in the Territories to wrest control of the separate schools away from the Church. Similarly, the growing number of French-Canadian settlers in eastern and northern Ontario found the educational institutions there inadequate to their requirements and adopted an aggressive programme to change them. As Professor Barber observes, "their intention was not to *defend* their rights but to *extend* their rights, not only to protect existing rights but also to secure additional ones."

There were, of course, obvious differences between the roles of the new settlers in the West and in Ontario. In the west the aggressive English-speaking new community was in a majority, exerting its influence throughout the province and the Territories. In Ontario the French-speaking new community was of the minority and could only exert its influence within a region of the province. In the West the reaction against the demands of the new community failed; in Ontario it succeeded. But the point remains. Large-scale shifts of population upset extant social patterns and institutions; the new communities judged the existing institutions inadequate and in their efforts to change them created the minority schools crises.

The second common theme in these essays is that the resolution of these crises was to be found only in politics. The Judicial Committee cases on the Manitoba schools made that point most sharply: when the constitutional niceties had been decided and the legal confusion cleared away, the problem remained, as void of solution as before and as dangerous for party unity within both provincial and federal parties as before. Put in its most cynical terms, whatever the lawyers and the judges decided, the children of the minority remained the pawns of the politicians. But as these essays reveal, the politicians were as much victims as they were manipulators of the minority schools crises. Action was forced upon them by their constituents. And, especially at the federal level, their responses, of necessity, had to be both delicate and compromising. In short, the minority schools crises between 1880 and 1920 were test cases of the state of French-English relations in Canada and in each case the provisions of the British North America Act could do no more than set the legal limits of their resolution. Such solutions as were found rested in what the politicians did and did not do.

The intensity of racist sentiment in these minority schools conflicts is the third theme common to these essays. The undoubted importance of denominational questions, the fact that the legal problems involved in these crises were all concerned with the rights and privileges of denominational schools, tends to obscure but cannot hide this ugly characteristic of the schools crises. In their not infrequent moments of candour many of the protagonists themselves confessed that race, not religion, was the basic issue. Dalton McCarthy told an audience in Barrie, in 1887, that "My own conviction is that it is not religion which is at the bottom of the matter but that it is race feeling. There is no feeling so strong – no feeling which all history proves so strong – as the feeling of race. . . . Do [the French] mix with us, assimilate with us, intermarry with us? Do they read our literature or learn our laws? No, everything with them is conducted on a French model; and while we may admire members of that race as individuals, yet as members of the body politic I say that they are a great danger to the Confederacy." The objective of the extremists among the majority was the elimination of the French Canadians' identity. The voice of the Orange Order, the *Sentinel*, commented in 1910 that "it is this refusal to assimilate that makes the French-Canadians so difficult to get along with." And for their part, the aim of L'Association Canadienne-Française d'Education d'Ontario, "la juste revendication de tous les droits des Canadiens-Français d'Ontario et l'infatigable surveillance de leurs intérêts," well expresses the defence of the minority against its loss of identity.

Finally, as the third theme suggests, the question implicit in all of

these essays is what is the nature of Canada itself? Was Canada
intended to be a nation of two cultures, of two nationalities? Surely
that is what the minority school crises of the period were fundament-
ally all about. It is to that central question that Professor Creighton
addresses himself in the first essay in this volume. His comments on
the minority schools problems in the West are instructive but of less
import than his general thesis which is presented with great force and
skill. He argues that in recent years "a group of politicians, lawyers,
historians and journalists, mainly French-Canadian but with some
English-Canadian associates" have given Confederation "a radically
new interpretation." In that interpretation, the "real essence of the
Canadian federal union is thus the cultural duality of Canada. And
Confederation becomes a compact between two cultures, two nations,
English and French." Professor Creighton, in a biting analysis of that
new interpretation, rejects its central assumptions about Confederation
and the nature of Canada. The remaining essays in this volume suggest
that the advocates of minority schools in Manitoba, Ontario, and the
North-West Territories, did not.

FURTHER READING
Book II of the government of Canada's *Report of the Royal Commission
on Bilingualism and Biculturalism* (Ottawa, 1968) summarizes the
commission's findings on the subject of education. Of particular importance is chapter III which emphasizes the language problem in the
minority schools crises in Canadian history. C. B. Sissons' *Bi-lingual
Schools in Canada* (Toronto, 1917) and *Church and State in Canadian
Education* (Toronto, 1959) are standard accounts. Chapter IV of D. A.
Schmeiser, *Civil Liberties in Canada* (London, 1964) is a good discussion of the legal and constitutional problems in the minority schools
crises and F. Henry Johnson, *A Brief History of Canadian Education*
(Toronto, 1968) places the crises in the context of a general survey of
Canadian educational history.

A thorough account of the Manitoba schools question is found in
W. L. Morton's *Manitoba: A History* (revised ed.; Toronto, 1968).
This may be supplemented by Lovell Clark's fine edition of documents
and readings, *The Manitoba Schools Question: Majority Rule or
Minority Rights?* (Toronto, 1968). For further reading on the controversy over bilingual schools in Ontario, see F. A. Walker, *Catholic
Education and Politics in Ontario* (Toronto, 1964) and the Ontario
government's *Report of the Royal Commission on Education in Ontario, 1950* (Toronto, 1950). A number of political biographies have
important discussions of the school crises in Manitoba, the Territories,
and Ontario. Among them are O. D. Skelton, *Life and Letters of Sir*

Wilfrid Laurier (2 vols.; Toronto, 1921), Joseph Schull, *Laurier, The First Canadian* (Toronto, 1965), J. W. Dafoe, *Clifford Sifton in Relation to His Times* (Toronto, 1931), Robert Rumilly, *Henri Bourassa* (Montreal, 1953) and Henry Borden, ed., *Sir Robert Laird Borden: His Memoirs* (2 vols.; Toronto, 1938).

The reaction in French Canada to the minority schools crises is assessed in the appropriate volumes of Robert Rumilly's multi-volume *Histoire de la Province de Québec* (Montreal, 1940–) and Mason Wade's *The French Canadians, 1760–1967* (2 vols.; Toronto, 1955). Ramsay Cook's perceptive book of essays, *Canada and the French Canadian Question* (Toronto, 1966) refers to the school crises in his discussion of the central problem of English-French relations in Canadian history. Especially important is chapter 9, "The Meaning of Confederation," which offers a different interpretation of the question posed by Professor Creighton in this volume.

John A. Macdonald, Confederation, and the Canadian West

D. G. CREIGHTON

Today, January 11, 1967, is the 152nd anniversary of the birth of John A. Macdonald; the centenary of Confederation is less than six months away; and in only three years from now the Province of Manitoba will be a hundred years old. It is appropriate for students of history to re-examine these major events of the past; and it is particularly important to do so at the present moment, for we are now confronted by a radically new interpretation of their meaning. Historians, of course, are always busy revising and modifying the accepted historical record; but I am not thinking of such minor changes in detail or emphasis.

The version of Confederation which has become current during the past few years is much more than this. It amounts, in fact, to a new theory of Canadian federalism, a theory which rests on the basic assumption that ethnic and cultural values are and ought to be recognized as fundamental in the life of the Canadian nation. The real essence of the Canadian federal union is thus the cultural duality of Canada. And Confederation becomes a compact between two cultures, two nations, English and French.

This interpretation, I have already suggested, is fairly new. The point deserves to be emphasized. In fact, the new version has been given expression mainly during the last six or, at most, the last ten years. Its increasing popularity among historians, writers, and journalists may, of course, be attributed in part to the interest in Canadian federalism which has been growing steadily as the centenary of Confederation approached. But though the centennial would naturally have revived an interest in Confederation, it would not necessarily have inspired a radical new interpretation of it. The real origins of the new theory are political; they lie in the rapid rise of French-Canadian nationalism which has come about since Jean Lesage in 1960 assumed power in Quebec. For the last half-dozen years a group of politicians, lawyers, historians and journalists, mainly French-Canadian but with some English-Canadian associates, have been disseminating a radically new view of Confederation and of French Canada's place in it. Their aims are varied and in some degree contradictory. On the one hand they have tried to improve the status and enlarge the rights of French Canadians in the nation as a whole; on the other, they have sought to emphasize the separateness and strengthen the autonomy of the Province of Quebec. At one and the same time they seem to believe in a

Reprinted from Historical and Scientific Society of Manitoba, *Transactions*, Series III, No. 23, 1966–67

bilingual, bicultural but united Canada, and a virtually independent Quebec, which, if it decides to remain in confederation at all, will have to be given a "special position" and may even become an "associate state".

Obviously, the realization of either or both these aims would mean a revolution in the present structure of Confederation. But Confederation, embodied in the law and custom of the constitution, is an inheritance from the past; and inevitably therefore, the French-Canadian nationalists and their English-Canadian associates have had to cope with the intractable problem of history. Like everybody who desires social and political change, or is merely interested in its possibility, they had to make up their minds about the past. Revolutionaries have realized this necessity long ago and they have evolved two different, and indeed quite contradictory methods of coming to terms with history. The "quiet revolutionaries" of Quebec appropriated both. The first method is to dismiss the past as irrelevant and meaningless for the present; the second is to identify the past with the revolutionary aims of the present. In other words, history can be rejected as a useless obstacle to the revolutionary programme; or it can be re-interpreted to provide a justification for it.

The case for the dismissal of the past is not our business tonight. But the historical re-interpretation of Confederation which the Quebec nationalists have been so persistently offering for the last six years is certainly worth examining. This is an historical society and I am an historian; and we are - or should be - interested in the use, or misuse, of history. Revolutionary re-interpretations of the past usually have a purpose. In this case, the object of the "quiet revolutionaries" was to back up a political programme with a new theory of federalism. The old view of confederation as a political union of several provinces must be broken down and discredited; and the conception of Canada as a cultural duality, as a partnership of two different cultures or "nations", must be established in its place. The fiction of duality was to be substituted for the fact of plurality. The true meaning of confederation, the French-Canadian nationalists argued, has been misunderstood and its essential spirit forgotten. Only on the surface can it be regarded as an agreement among several provinces; in reality it was a compact between the two cultures, the two nations, English and French, of Canada.

There is very little aid or comfort for the believers of this theory in what we know of the aims and intentions of the Fathers of Confederation. There is no support for it at all in the lean, spare phrases of the Quebec resolutions or the British North America Act. It is obvious that the last thing the Fathers of Confederation wanted to do was to perpetuate duality; they hoped, through confederation, to escape from it forever. They had seen enough, and more than enough, of duality in the old province of Canada. There it had paralyzed governments and prevented progress for a quarter of a century. The new Dominion of Canada was to be organized, as the arrangements for the Senate make quite clear, not as a duality but as a triumvirate of three divisions: Quebec, Ontario, and Atlantic provinces as a group. The distinctive cultural features of French Canada — its language, civil code, and educational system — were confirmed in those parts of Canada in which they had already become established by law or custom. But that was all. They were not extended in their application to Ontario or to the Maritime provinces. There was nothing in the Quebec Resolutions or the British North America Act which remotely approached a general declaration of principle that Canada was to be a bilingual or bicultural nation.

The evidence against the two-nation theory of Confederation is so overwhelming that some of its advocates have been driven back upon a secondary line of defence. The bicultural compact, they admit, was only a "tacit" or "implicit" agreement, or a "moral" commitment, when the British North America Act was framed. But later, when Canada expanded westward and the Hudson's Bay Company territories were taken over, the Fathers of Confederation honoured the moral commitments and took care to provide that the new western domain should become the joint possession, on equal terms, of both English and French-speaking Canadians. The first Conservative government after confederation established Separate Schools and gave legal status to the French language in Manitoba. The first Liberal government after confederation did exactly the same for the North-West Territories. It was a basic national policy, deliberately adopted, carefully carried out, concurred in by both parties.

This, in short, is the theory of confederation as a bicultural compact applied to Manitoba and the North-West Territories. What is its truth when tested by the actual events of the time? This is the problem which I should like to examine with you tonight.

II

John A. Macdonald was above everything else a nation builder. The union of the original British North American colonies was the first of his two greatest achievements; the expansion and integration of the new Dominion on a continental scale was the second. He was an expansionist; but he was also a realist. His purpose was to ensure that Canada would not be despoiled of her great territorial inheritance on the North American continent; he was absolutely determined that, as he himself put it, "the United States should not get behind us by right or by force and intercept the route to the Pacific". In his mind there was no doubt about Canada's ultimate destiny; but at the same time he was equally convinced that Canada should assume its great heritage slowly and prudently, a step at a time, by one firm stage after another. Even as late as March, 1865 he would have preferred to see Rupert's Land and the North-West Territories remain a crown colony under imperial control. He soon realized, however, that the march of events could not be so deliberate as he had hoped. Great Britain's urge to withdraw from her North American commitments, the British government's desire that Canada should take over its responsibilities in the north-west, and the threat of American northward expansion all helped to convince him that there could be no more delay. In the spring of 1869 the bargain with the Hudson's Bay Company was finally concluded and Canada prepared to assume the assets and liabilities of its new western Dominion.

At this point it should be emphasized that Macdonald was still trying to hold fast, as far as he was able, to his original policy respecting the North-West. He had been compelled, far earlier than he had wanted to, to assume responsibility for Rupert's Land and the Territories; but he knew very well that the problem of their government and future development was a difficult one and he had no intention of risking a hasty solution to it. The bill which he introduced in the Canadian House of Commons late in May, 1869 was characteristically entitled "For the Temporary Government of Rupert's Land". It deserves far more attention than it has yet received. It is the only document that embodies the Conservative cabinet's original policy respecting the north-west; it expresses Macdonald's original intentions, his first tentative provisional plans. And it is obvious from its few brief clauses that he was trying to keep as closely as possible to the idea of a Crown colony, the idea which he had proposed as little as four years before. The North-West was to be governed, not as a province but as a territory, by a lieutenant-governor and a small nominated council. The existing laws were to continue until altered; the public officers were to retain their posts until it was ordered otherwise. Nothing was to be changed in a hurry. Nothing new was to be introduced at once. There was no mention of either schools or languages.

Now it is usually assumed that this whole provincial plan of government was invalidated by the Red River Rising of 1869-70. It is also usually taken for granted — even less justifiably, it seems to me — that the Manitoba Act of 1870 was the only natural result, the logical and inevitable constitutional consequence of the rising. Both those assumptions, I am convinced, badly need a critical examination; and the examination ought to begin by making a clear distinction between the Red River community on the one hand and the military dictatorship of Louis Riel on the other. There is no doubt whatever about the kind of government which the Red River community would have liked to see established in the north-west. Their wishes were democratically determined in the debates of the Convention which met at Fort Garry in mid-winter 1870; and the results were embodied in the resolutions of the second "List of Rights". If this second list — the one document in which the constitutional preferences of the whole Red River community are faithfully recorded — had formed the basis of the negotiations at Ottawa, the Manitoba Act of 1870 would have been a very different statute. The Convention, against the opposition and to the intense indignation of Riel, decided against provincial status, at least for the time being. It requested equality for the English and French languages in the legislature and the courts; but it made no mention of separate or confessional schools. If the wishes of the Convention and the terms of the second "List of Rights" had been followed in drafting the Manitoba Act, there would have been no very serious departure from Macdonald's *Act for the Temporary Government of Rupert's Land* of the previous year.

But this moderate and sensible constitutional settlement was not to be. Riel was determined to prevent it. An adroit and ruthless dictator, he had no intention of permitting democracy to have its own way at Red River. His terms for the union with Canada had been openly and emphatically rejected by the Convention; but at the same time, as a final reluctant concession in the interest of political conciliation in the Settlement, the Convention had confirmed the provisional government and elected Riel as its president. At once and with purposeful energy he took over control of the negotiations with Canada. He quickly nominated Ritchot and Alfred Scott, who, he felt confident, would support his own private plans for the future of the north-west; and he persuaded the reluctant Convention to accept them as two of the three emissaries to the Canadian government. He then proceeded to make short work of the Convention's "List of Rights". The wishes of the Red River community, where they differed from his claims for his own people, the *Métis*, meant nothing whatever to him. In two quite new and increasingly detailed "Lists of Rights", drawn up in private by Riel and his lay and clerical advisers, the delegates sent to Ottawa were instructed to insist that the North-West should enter Confederation, not as a Territory, but as a Province. It must have, they demanded, an elaborate provincial constitution with an absurdly top-heavy bi-cameral legislature, including a little senate on the model of Quebec. It must also have a system of sectarian or confessional schools, again on the Quebec model. This, if you like, was a demand that biculturalism should prevail on the prairies and that French and English institutions should be combined in the government of the north-west; but it was neither a demand that was made by the community at Red River nor a plan proposed by the government of Ottawa. It was a claim exacted by Riel's dictatorship.

Why did Macdonald accept it? Why did he consent to impose such an elaborate constitution upon such an immature colony? How was he persuaded to settle all the basic institutions of a community which had not yet had time to develop its real and permanent character? The answers to these questions can never be absolutely certain, for the conclusive evidence is lacking; but the probabilities at all events are very clear. The pressures in favour of a quick settlement in the north-west were inescapable and compelling. Macdonald's foremost aim was to ensure, at almost any cost, Canada's continental destiny, her unobstructed expansion from the Atlantic to the Pacific Ocean. His greatest fear was that the United States, by deliberate policy or tragic accident, might prevent the achievement of these natural limits. He knew only too well that the acrimonious disputes which had arisen between Great Britain and the United States during the American

Civil War had not yet been settled. There was evidence that both
President Grant and Secretary of State Hamilton Fish were annexa-
tionists, prepared to use any method short of war to acquire all or part
of British America. And finally it was clear from the beginning, that the
American expansionists at St. Paul, Minnesota — the "Yankee Wire-
pullers", Macdonald called them — were eager to exploit the rising
at Red River, and that American citizens in the settlement were deep in
Riel's councils. So long as the provisional government continued, so long
as the future of the British American north-west remained uncertain
and confederation was still incomplete, the threat of American intervention hung over Canada's future.

A quick settlement was urgently necessary. And its character by this
time was fixed and virtually unalterable. Appeasement on any terms
meant in fact appeasement on the terms demanded by the fanatical
emissaries from Red River, backed up by Cartier and his French
Canadian "Bleu" followers, and supported by Sir Clinton Murdoch of
the British Colonial Office. It is true, of course, that the Canadian
government refused to yield to Riel's vainglorious and incredible
demand that the entire North-West enter Confederation as a single
province; and it is also true that the request for provincial control of
public lands was likewise rejected. Macdonald could limit boundaries
and withhold lands, but within the restricted area of the new Province
of Manitoba he had to accept a bilingual and bicultural system of rights
and institutions. "The French", Sir Stafford Northcote observed, "are
earnestly bent upon the establishment of a French and Catholic power
in the North-West to counteract the great preponderance of Ontario".
Their purpose was to fix the character and institutions of the new
province at a time when French-speaking Roman Catholics formed a
large part of its population, and therefore at the most favourable
moment for preparing defences against the approaching influx of
Protestant, English-speaking settlers.

III

The Manitoba Act did not represent the carrying-out of a solemn
commitment to biculturalism which had been made at Confederation.
It was not drafted in fulfilment of an ideal conception of what Canada
should be; it was, to a very large extent, imposed simply by the force
of circumstance. In 1869-70 a particular set of circumstances, including
some very frightening external circumstances, had practically dictated
a hasty policy of appeasement. But these circumstances were exceptional and transitory; they did not reappear in quite the same powerful constitution; and as a result the main argument in favour of
biculturalism lost most of its force. This would not have mattered, of
course, if the Fathers of Confederation had really felt morally committed to the ideal of a bilingual and bicultural Canada, to the conception of two nations in the Canadian national state. But the simple
truth is that they did not. The French language and French-Canadian

institutions had not been given legal status in any province of the original union outside Quebec; and no attempt had been made to establish the equality of the two cultures in any of the provinces that entered Confederation after Manitoba. The Manitoba Act did not lay down a national bicultural pattern which was solemnly confirmed and carefully followed thereafter. When British Columbia and Prince Edward Island joined the union, nobody so much as mentioned the great moral commitment to biculturalism.

The exception to this consistent record is, of course, the North-West Territories. And it is a very dubious exception which effectively proves the rule. It was not until the session of 1875, nearly five years after this passage of the Manitoba Act, that the Parliament of Canada finally got around to setting up a system of organized government in the western territory beyond the new province of Manitoba. The main feature of the North-West Territories bill, which the new Prime Minister Alexander Mackenzie introduced in the Commons, was a rather complicated set of clauses providing for the gradual introduction of elected members in the North-West Council as the population of the region increased. The bill contained no reference to separate or confessional schools, and no provision for the French language. If this silence could have been made to appear as a betrayal of a recognized bicultural compact, it is obvious that the Conservative opposition, in which several of the Fathers of Confederation were sitting, would have been quick to grasp the opportunity of so doing. But the Conservative member sat silent. And it was left to Edward Blake, who was not a Father of Confederation and knew nothing whatever at first hand of its purposes or principles, to move, in amendment, that separate or confessional schools should be established in the territories.

Why did Blake take up the cause of what he called "religious instruction" in the north-west? On the record, there was no reason to expect him to show any particular sympathy for the Roman Catholic *Métis* of the prairies; on the contrary, he was thought to share the critical views of *Canada First* and its representatives at Red River, Mair and Schultz. In 1871, when he had been leader of the opposition in the Ontario legislature, Blake had moved a resolution demanding that the "murderer" Riel should be brought to justice; and in the following year, after he had formed the first Liberal government in Ontario, he introduced a similar resolution offering a five thousand dollar reward for the arrest and conviction of the "murderers" of Thomas Scott. Undoubtedly he had gained a good deal of political capital from these astute moves; and political capital may well have been what he was after in the session of 1875. He was not a member of Mackenzie's government; he had been angling deviously for Mackenzie's post as Prime Minister; he was critical of Mackenzie's policies and determined to block his railway bill; and he was embarrassing him at every turn.

It was in this curious way, and with this unexpected sponsorship, that separate schools found their way into the North-West Territories

Act of 1875. The grant of legal status to the French language, which
was made when the statute was amended in 1877, came about in an
even stranger and more accidental fashion. It was not a government
amendment at all; it was proposed by a private member in the Senate.
And the speech with which David Mills, the Minister of the Interior,
greeted this amendment when it was brought down to the Commons
effectively destroys the odd notion that the promotion of biculturalism
on the prairies was the settled policy of Liberal as well as Conservative
governments. Mills reminded the members that the dominant language
of the region was Cree; he thought the North-West council was the only
body that could properly settle the question of official languages. He
regretted the Senate amendment; and he reluctantly accepted it because
otherwise it would be impossible to get the revised statute through
Parliament before the end of the session.

We are now in a position, it seems to me, to come to certain con-
clusions. The bicultural compact theory of Confederation as applied to
Manitoba and the North-West Territories cannot be sustained. The
idea of a solemn commitment to biculturalism, accepted in principle
and deliberately implemented by both parties, is simply not borne out
by the facts. The west did not get its institutions in accordance with the
provisions of some long-range plan; on the contrary, the process was
characterized throughout by accident and improvisation. The pressure
of circumstances, the influence of certain powerful political interests,
and the ambition of a few key personalities, all combined to force a
series of hasty and ill-considered decisions; and the result was the
abandonment of Macdonald's plan for the gradual development of
government in the North-West and the premature establishment of an
elaborate and cumbrous constitution. This attempt to fix the political
institutions of the west before immigration and the growth of population had determined its true and permanent character was a mistake
for which the whole of Canada paid dearly. By 1890 — only twenty
years after the Manitoba Act and fifteen years after the North-West
Territories Act — the west had outgrown the inappropriate constitution that had been imposed upon it. It began suddenly and uncom-
promisingly to change the status of the French language and the
character of its schools. The violent controversy that followed lasted
for more than a quarter of a century; and it ended in the virtual
extinction of biculturalism in the Canadian west.

This is an episode in our history which should not be forgotten. We
should all remember it when we come to read the forthcoming report
of the Royal Commission on Bilingualism and Biculturalism. The
commission may possibly recommend constitutional changes designed to
improve the position of the French language and of French-Canadian
culture throughout the nation, including the west. These proposals
should be judged critically in the light of history; and with the aid of
the same clear light, westerners should examine the historical theory
by which these proposals will probably be justified. The idea of a bicultural compact, of the two-nation state, has got much of its currency

and its vogue during a period of profound revolution in Quebec; and this very fact ought to make it suspect. New historical interpretations which make their appearance in revolutionary times are usually the result, not of the search for truth, but of the need for historical justification. They are invented — or partly invented — to supply historical authority for a program of radical changes. Canadians on the whole are badly equipped to protect themselves against this kind of propaganda. For they are not as historically minded as the English, and, unlike the Americans, they have not been brought up in a thorough knowledge of their own history. They cling to old myths, and are easily sold new and spurious inventions. It would be a tragedy if, at this most critical period of their history, they were led to damage their future irretrievably through a serious misunderstanding of their past.

Manitoba Schools and Canadian Nationality, 1890-1923

W. L. MORTON

I

PRIOR TO the entry of the Red River Colony into the Canadian federation, the population and schools of the colony had been English and French, Protestant and Catholic. The duality of nationality and education was given formal recognition in the Manitoba Act in 1870 which granted official status to the French and English languages and to denominational schools. In the course of time, however, the duality of language and education was challenged by the growth of a British-Ontario majority and by the immigration of people who were neither English nor French; and during the period with which this paper is concerned the principle of duality was abandoned.[1] This process was finally completed by the enactment of the School Act of 1916 which established English as the sole official language and created a secular public school system.[2]

II

The precarious balance of English and Protestant, French and Catholic, elements in the West rested, not only on the constitutional safeguards of the British North America Act 1867 and the Manitoba Act 1870, but also upon the numerical equality of the two groups. This equality, however, soon disappeared in the face of the comparatively large and rapid inflow of settlers from Ontario and the British Isles. "Le nombre va nous faire défaut" wrote Taché sadly, "et comme sous notre système constitutionel les nombres sont la force, nous allons nous trouver à la merci de ceux qui ne nous aiment pas"[3] The Roman Catholic clergy fought to preserve the language and culture of Old Quebec in the West, and with aid from Quebec and from France, they encouraged the foundation of compact French-speaking parishes both in Manitoba and the North West Territories.

It was, however, a losing battle, and in 1890 the defences of French culture were breached when Manitoba became a province of municipalities rather than a province of parishes.[4] The agents of commercial civilization, the railway and the grain trade, had swept away

[1]See Noël Bernier, *Fannystelle* (*Publié sous les aupices de la Société Historique de Saint-Boniface, Manitoba,* n.d. [1939]) p. 162.
[2]See Pamphlets, Hon. R. S. Thornton, *Bi-Lingual Schools: An Address in the Legislature on January* 12th, 1916. (Department of Education Winnipeg, 1916) p. 11.
[3]Dom Benoit, *Vie de Monseigneur Taché,* (Montreal, 1904) II, 195-196. Taché wrote to Sir George Cartier in 1869, "J'ai toujours redouté l'entree du Nord-Ouest dans la Conféderation parce que j'ai toujours cru que l'élément français catholique serait sacrifié . . . " *Ibid.,* II, 17.
[4]See C. B. Sissons, *Egerton Ryerson, His Life and Letters,* (Toronto, 1947) II, 270.

Reprinted from Canadian Historical Association, *Report*, 1951

the old order. In that year the legislature of Manitoba, controlled by the Liberal party under Premier Thomas Greenway, abolished both the official use of the French language in the province and the dual system of separate denominational schools.

For these drastic acts, carried out after nineteen years of comparative satisfaction with the separate school system and two official languages,[5] there were, in the main, two particular and two general causes. The anti-Catholic agitation which D'Alton McCarthy led in Ontario, in reaction against the Jesuits Estates Act of 1888 and inspired by the fear of *political Catholicism,* was carried to Manitoba in August of 1889. There it awakened a sympathetic response in the new English and Protestant settlements west of the Red River Valley. The agitation neatly coincided with the political embarrassment of the provincial Liberal party, which after the agitation against the railway "monopoly" of the Canadian Pacific Railway, had failed to procure a lowering of freight rates in a contract with the Northern Pacific Railway. To divert attention from their failure, the Liberals had already determined to take up the amendment of the separate school system. "Fighting Joe" Martin's famous outburst on the platform with McCarthy at Portage la Prairie committed the Government to going much farther along the same road, to establish a system of secular public schools and to abolish the official use of the French language.[6]

These two particular causes brought into play two general causes which had been shaping beneath the surface of politics as the settlement of the West proceeded. One was the difficulty and cost of organizing and maintaining municipal and educational institutions on the frontier at the speed competitive settlement required. The burden of local taxes for local improvements and schools was heavy on settlers engaged in making farms in new territory.[7] The dual system of schools threatened to increase this burden—threatened rather than did, because, as the English and French settlers in Manitoba were segregated, few school districts had in fact to provide separate schools.[8] Related to the question of cost and also related to the question of duality, was the growing feeling that a country of heterogeneous population, as Manitoba had become with the formation of Mennonite and Icelandic colonies within its borders, should develop a uniform

[5]While there was an outburst in 1875 following the first Ontario immigration after 1870, against the school system and the official use of French, there was in fact little public criticism of either until the late summer of 1889. The point is exhaustively established by A. E. Clague in "The Manitoba School Question, 1890-1896". (Unpublished M.A. thesis, University of Manitoba, 1939) chaps. I-III.

[6]P.A.M., Greenway Papers, Joseph Martin to Thomas Greenway, August 6, 1889; also J. S. Willison, *Sir Wilfrid Laurier and the Liberal Party,* (Toronto, 1903) II, 202.

[7]This point is too easily lost sight of in the controversy over principles. See John S. Ewart, *The Manitoba School Question,* (Toronto, 1894) 246-247; also *Canada, House of Commons Debates,* 1897, I, 371-374. The later phases of the school question in Manitoba and the events leading to the formation of the United Church of Canada enforce the point.

[8]Ewart, *Manitoba School Question,* 63; address before Governor-General in Council, Jan. 21, 1893.

nationality through the agency of a "national" school system.[9] It
was this immigration, neither English nor French, and either Protestant or Catholic, which began to complicate the working of the
principle of duality in Manitoba.   It was used, by those who ques-
tioned the principle itself and feared the political power of the Catholic
Church, to justify the abolition of the dual system of education and
the denial of the concept of dual nationality.

    With the events of the litigation and political controversy caused
by the school question from 1890 to 1896 this paper need not be
concerned.   Suffice it to say that the result was the Laurier-Greenway
Compromise of 1896, which was enacted by the Manitoba Legislature
in 1897 as an amendment to the School Act of 1890.   By the amendment religious teaching, in defined circumstances, was permitted in the
public schools from 3:30 to 4 p.m., with a conscience clause which
permitted parents to have their children excused from such teaching.
The amendment also provided that when ten or more pupils spoke
French (or any language other than English) instruction should be
"in French (or such other language) and English upon the bi-lingual
system".   The bi-lingual clause was not directed to circumstances in
Manitoba, where the new immigration was just beginning, but to
political circumstances in Ontario and Quebec.   The concession of
teaching in French was designed to please Quebec, the concession of
teaching in a language other than French was designed to prevent
criticism in Ontario of a grant of equality to the French language
alone.[10]   It is also to be noted that the amendment of 1897 did nothing
to repair the omission from the Act of 1890 of any clause providing
for compulsory attendance.[11]   The public school system of Manitoba

[9]P.A.M., Manitoba School Case (clippings from contemporary press) 1, 90.
Resolution of Grand Lodge (Orange) of Western Ontario; " . . . separate schools
. . . perpetuate an improper union between church and state; . . . they do not
teach that the duty of every good citizen is to give his first loyalty to the nation
in which he lives . . . "; Gladstone Age, Apr. 17, 1895, J. W. Armstrong at public
meeting on school question: "Where we have so many different nationalities, it is
necessary to have some time to bind them together and blend all their characteristics in one common nationality"; Winnipeg Tribune, (clipping) 1895, "Is Manitoba Right?":   "If public education has been found necessary in a country like
Britain, the necessity is greatly emphasized in a new community like Manitoba,
with its heterogeneous and polyglot population, and the great diversity of intelli-
gence and ideas which characterizes its yet unassimilated elements."
    For a direct challenge to the principle of duality, see F. C. Wade, The Mani-
toba School Question, (Winnipeg, 1895) 51; "It cannot be conducive to our
national welfare to bring up the two great sections of our population apart from
each other."   The view of John S. Ewart and James Fisher, that a school system
at once "national" and "separate" was possible, commanded little sympathy on
either side of the controversy.
    [10]P.A.M., Manitoba Debates, (F.P.) 1916, 8; J. W. Dafoe, Clifford Sifton in
Relation to His Times (Toronto, 1931) 98.
    [11]The explanation of the omission of clauses providing for enforcement of
attendance given by Premier R. P. Roblin in the Legislature in 1914 and 1915 may
be accepted.   Roblin was an independent member of the Legislature in 1890, and
the bill of 1890 as amended in committee is in the files of the Legislature of Manitoba, with the attendance section struck out and initialled "C.S.", just as Roblin
described it in 1914 and 1915.   (See P.A.M., Manitoba Debates, (F.P.) 1914,
28-30, and Manitoba Debates (Trib.), 1915, 72).   Roblin said that Attorney-
General Martin, who drew up the bill, had included clauses providing for attendance.   On advice from D'Alton McCarthy, however, he had them struck out in
committee.   The chairman of that committee was Clifford Sifton.   It was feared

in 1897 was one in which, because of the right of Catholics to separate private schools, attendance was voluntary.

III

The passage of the Compromise of 1897 was followed in 1899 by the defeat of the Liberal Party in the provincial election of that year, a defeat in which the Compromise played some part. The accession to power of the Conservative party did not lead to the repeal or amendment of the Compromise. However the administration of the school law now lay with men who were not wholly sympathetic with its terms.[12] The Roblin Government maintained the "national school" system intact in principle and fact, yet in its administration made all possible concessions to the French and Catholics. In rural French parishes the results were satisfactory to the French; only in Winnipeg and St. Boniface did Catholics suffer actual hardship from the operation of the School Act.

Grave and growing difficulties, however, were encountered in the administration of the public school system in the newly settled districts along the northern and eastern frontiers of Manitoba. These were the years of the great immigration into the West, a great part of which came from east central Europe. In 1897 the three language groups of Manitoba were English, French and German; a fourth, the Icelandic, accepted public education in English while maintaining the mother tongue in the home and Icelandic press. By 1911, many other groups had been added, of which two, the Polish and the Ukrainian, were devoted to the maintenance of their native languages.[13] Moreover, of these groups the Poles and many of the Germans were Roman Catholics and to them the ministrations of the Church, led by Archbishop Langevin of St. Boniface, were naturally extended. The Ukrainians were mainly Greek Catholics. They had come without their native clergy and they therefore invited evangelisation by both the Protestant churches and the Church of Rome.

The great immigration, and the still active resentment of the Catholic clergy and of the lay leaders of the Manitoban French towards the school law, led to an increased emphasis on the bi-lingual provision of the school law. They also perpetuated the denominational hostility which had done so much to provoke the School Act of 1890. The French of course insisted on their right to instruction in the mother tongue; the Germans, both the Old Colony Mennonites and newcomers did so too; the Poles and Ukrainians soon learned, from the politicians not least, to do the same. The result was to

that compulsion would destroy the constitutional ground on which the bill was based, namely that the Catholics had a right to private and voluntary denominational schools, but not to separate schools supported by public funds. To compel the children of Catholic parents to attend the public schools would violate this right.

[12]The provincial premier after 1900, R. P. Roblin, had opposed both the School Act of 1890 and the amendment of 1897; the Conservative platform of 1899 had called for the freeing of the school systems "from party politics by the establishment of an independent board of education"; P.A.M., Pamphlets, Record of the Roblin Government, 1900-1909, 5.

[13]The composition of the population of Manitoba in 1911 was as follows: British, 266,415; French, 30,944; German, 34,530; Austro-Hungarian, 39,665; Polish, 12,310; Scandinavian, 16,419; and smaller groups, to a total of 55,311; Canada Year Book 1912, 24.

demonstrate that, under the new conditions, the bi-lingual system of 1897 was unworkable.[14]

As if these difficulties were not sufficiently harmful, there was also the lack of a school-attendance law. The lack had engaged the attention of the Roblin Government in 1900. It then and later, on legal advice, accepted the view that a compulsory attendance law would violate the constitutional rights of Catholics to separate private schools and re-open the school question. Accordingly, the administration decided to achieve its object by way of police legislation, rather than by altering the school law. In 1909 it amended the Children's Act.[15] The defects of this legislation were that delinquency had to be proved before children could be compelled to attend school. When the Act was tightened in 1914, however, and the Department of Education directed enforcement through its own truancy officers, the average school attendance in the Province began to rise. The advantages of central administration overcame the defects of the law.

Because of these difficulties and deficiencies, the school administration of the Roblin Government came under ever sharpening criticism, and the Liberal opposition made the most of the Government's embarrassment. The criticism from English Protestants was intensified by the passage of the ambiguous Coldwell amendments of 1912. These amendments, which seemed to permit the separation of Protestant and Catholic children in the larger schools, had coincided with the extension of Manitoba's boundaries, and with them of the jurisdiction of the School Act. Whatever the meaning of the amendments, they aroused strong resentment among the Orangemen of Manitoba.[16] The provincial Liberals, who had campaigned for reform of the school system in 1910, in 1914 included in their platform pledges to maintain unimpaired the national school system of 1897. They proposed to provide educational facilities for all children in the Province and to make adequate teaching of English obligatory in all public schools. In a carefully drawn plank the party undertook "to provide for a measure of compulsory education, which, while respecting the personal rights and religious convictions of the individual, shall make it obligatory on parents and guardians of all children that such children shall receive a proper elementary education, *either by attendance at the public schools, or by such substitute within the choice of*

[14]For an informed contemporary description of the operation of the bi-lingual section, see C. B. Sissons, *Bi-lingual Schools in Canada* (Toronto, 1917) pp. 116-155. See also R. Fletcher, "The Language Problem in Manitoba Schools," *papers read before Historical and Scientific Society of Manitoba* III (6) (Winnipeg, 1851) 55-56. Dr. Fletcher was a member of the Department of Education from 1903, and Deputy-Minister of Education, 1908-1939.

[15]This account is based on the defence of the government policy by Premier Roblin and the Minister of Education, Hon. George Coldwell, in moving amendments of the Truancy Act in 1914; P.A.M., *Manitoba Debates*, 1915 (T.) 72.

[16]*Canada, H. of C. Debates*, 1911-12, III, 4839-4925 and 4934-4973. No direct connection between the boundary extension of 1912 and the amendments has, to the writer's knowledge, ever been established. But that the amendments were a fumbling attempt to conciliate Catholic feeling without arousing Protestant resentment seems probable; see A. G. Morice, *Vie de Monseigneur Langevin*, pp. 284-285. In further confirmation of this assumption, it is of interest to know that the amendments were drafted outside the Province of Manitoba.

the parents as shall attain this end." The party also pledged itself to
increase the provincial grants to rural schools, and repeal the Coldwell
amendments. They thus undertook to make the system of 1897
work, and at the same time they hoped to evade the constitutional
difficulty with respect to compulsory attendance by allowing parents a
substitute acceptable to the Department of Education.[17] The religious
rights of Catholic parents were to be respected; but there was no
suggestion of compromise on the principle of duality.

IV

The Liberal party failed to win the election of 1914, but came
to power in 1915 when the Roblin Government fell for reasons
unconnected with the administration of education. The new government of Premier T. C. Norris was emphatically a reform administration and in the Minister of Education, Dr. R. S. Thornton,
possessed an administrator of clear purpose and unflinching will. A
school-attendance act, correcting the existing anomalous situation, was
carried through the legislature in the session of 1916 without opposition.[18] The bill to repeal the bi-lingual section, No. 258, of the
Public School Act, however, provoked bitter opposition from the
French-speaking members, and the only Ukrainian member, of the
Legislature. It was, in fact, the only measure introduced by the government during the session which led to a division in the legislature.
The bitterness expressed by the French members was natural enough.
The Liberal Party, in its platform of 1914 and during the election
campaigns had committed itself only to the enforcement of adequate
instruction in English thereby implying the retention of the principle
of the bi-lingual system and the use of administrative methods to improve English language teaching. Now the party proposed to do
away with the whole principle of bi-lingual instruction.

In moving the deletion of the bi-lingual clause from the School
Act the Minister of Education explained that until the autumn of
1915, he had hoped to achieve the purpose of the government, that is,
to enforce adequate instruction in English, by administrative means.
That hope had been defeated by the mandatory character of the legislation of 1897, the conditions revealed by a special report on the
bi-lingual schools, and by an increase in the petitions for bi-lingual
teaching. The problem had ceased to be, as in 1897, a peripheral
one; one quarter of the schools with one sixth of the enrolment were
bi-lingual in 1915. The Deputy-Minister, Robert Fletcher, had
reported that the situation was nearly out of hand. In short, it had
been proved to the Minister's satisfaction that adequate instruction in
English could be provided only by making English the sole language
of instruction.[19]

Over and above these administrative considerations, it is to be
noted, there were the mounting racial sentiment of the war years and
the effect of the powerful and sustained campaign by the *Manitoba*

[17]P.A.M., Pamphlets, *Liberal Platform of 1914.* (Saint-Boniface, 1919). The
legal thought behind the substitute clause was later expounded by Attorney-General
A. B. Hudson, subsequently a member of the Supreme Court of Canada, P.A.M.,
Manitoba Debates, (*F.P.*) 1916, 28.
[18]Much of the benefit of this act was, however, lost by placing its administration in the hands of local officials.
[19]P.A.M., *Manitoba Debates,* (*F.P.*) 1916, 5-7.

Free Press against the bi-lingual system. And it is to be remembered
that the dispute in Ontario over Regulation 17 was at its height, that
Bourassa had forced Laurier to take up the cause of Nationalism in
Quebec, and that the conscription issue was looming.

The Minister convinced his colleagues of the need for legislation
but to convince the caucus of his party was more difficult. The meeting which considered the proposed change of policy lasted until the
small hours. Influential leaders sought to preserve for the French
language a status similar to that which it possessed in Saskatchewan.
It was reported that the French members refused to accept the concession of instruction in French as well as English, but demanded the
re-establishment of separate schools as of 1889. Compromise was
impossible, and Thornton's proposal was adopted.[20] The two French
Liberal members, P. A. Talbot and J. P. Dumas, then broke with the
Liberal party.

The grounds of opposition were manifest and were debated at
length in the Legislature. The French members of the Legislature,
both Liberal and Conservative, declared that the rights of the French
had been betrayed by the Liberal party. That party had pledged
itself to maintain the compromise of 1897. In office it spurned its
public and unequivocal undertakings. The Premier himself, it was
charged, had given pledges, both in writing and in speech, that the
rights of the French would be respected. The charges were met fairly
by Norris and Thornton, but the bitter sense of betrayal felt by the
French members drove them on to assert the whole claim of their
people, their historical, moral and constitutional right to have denominational schools and to have equality of the French language
with English; to assert, in short, the principle of duality. "If any
single member expects the English to assimilate the French in this
Dominion," said Talbot, "I might give them the friendly advice to
disabuse themselves [sic.]. The French are a distinctive race, and we
will not be assimilated, whether you like it or not. The sooner you
know it the better. We have been given our rights as a separate
nationality and we will hold them."[21] The bill, the French members
declared, was a violation of the "pact", or "treaty" of Confederation,
which had recognized the equal and distinct status of the French in
Canada. "The French and Catholic population of Manitoba," declared a protest prepared by a committee of the Manitoban French
and tabled in the Legislature "have by natural law, by the title of first
occupancy, by solemn treaties, by the B.N.A. Act, by the pact
solemnly entered into by the Delegates of the Territory of Assiniboia
and the North-West Territories with the Dominion of Canada, by
the Manitoba Act and subsequent legislation, rights and privileges
which have been violated by the Legislature of Manitoba."[22] To the
embittered and bewildered French, the bill was "an attempt on our
national life".[23]

[20]The reports of this caucus are, as is usual, meagre. P.A.M., *Manitoba
Debates*, (F.P.) 1916, pp. 44-45. The substance of the Reports is accepted here,
because it is supported by the subsequent debates.
[21]P.A.M., *Manitoba Debates* (F.P.) 1916, 31. Talbot was reproached in the
debate with being a "nationalist" and a "separatist", but denied that he was a
Nationalist of Bourassa's school. He was, in fact, at that time a Laurier Liberal.
[22]*Canadian Annual Review*, 1916, 673.
[23]*Ibid.*, 1921, 774.

The reply of the government was that the French language had no constitutional standing in Manitoba. The religious rights of Roman Catholics were not touched, were indeed not involved. Some members, and the local press, admitted the special status, on historical and moral grounds, of the French language. But there was no obligation, it was asserted, to respect that status, as the French had neither accepted the Compromise of 1897 nor an offer of special treatment.[24] By standing out for their whole claim, based on natural law and the constitution, and for the retention of the bi-lingual system of 1897, they had identified themselves with the other language groups, the Germans, Ukrainians and Poles and menaced the Legislature with the re-opening of the school question in its entirety. By their refusal to compromise, the French of Manitoba had brought down on their cause the fate preparing for the other non-English languages.[25] As J. D Baskerville reminded the Legislature, "the battle at Babel had broken the contract".[26] The reply of the government and its supporters was made, not unsympathetically but very firmly; for the general conviction in the Legislature was that the operation of the bi-lingual clause had threatened the very foundations of Canadian nationality in Manitoba. It was imperative that the danger be removed, "if a common citizenship were to be built up in Canada".[27]

Immigration into the West had introduced a third element into the crucible, a third element which by 1916 had affected both the distinct and formed nationalities of 1870. Because the newcomers were assimilated to the English group, the influx reduced the French to a minority and led to the loss of the rights held by them from 1870 to 1890. It also affected the English group by the insistence of many of the immigrants both on assimilation to the English group in public life and on the retention of their mother tongue and culture in private life. In this trend the Icelandic and Scandinavian peoples led. Both the Icelandic members of the Legislature in 1916 supported the abolition of bi-lingual teaching and one of them, Hon. T. H. Johnson, declared: "We admit, and we all must admit, that there is only one nationality possible in the future, a Canadian nationality, and we claim the privilege of becoming merged in that, and the privilege of contributing towards that, whatever national characteristics we may possess."[28] While rejecting the principle of duality, Manitoba, out of the confusion created by the bi-lingual clause and the great immigration, was groping towards a combination of political uniformity with cultural plurality.

In the end the abolition of the bi-lingual system was carried by thirty-eight votes to eight. The opposition was made up of two dissident French Liberals, one Ukrainian member, and the Conservative Opposition of five, of whom two were French speaking. The decisive character of the vote settled the issue. Although opposition flared up briefly in 1917 when the Government proposed to make the

[24]*Ibid.*, 8, 46-47, 49-51, 53-55; also *Manitoba Debates*, (F.P.) 1920, p. 46, in which A. B. Hudson reviewed the controversy; " . . . it seemed to him what had been done was the only thing that could be done."

[25]*Winnipeg Free Press Library*, Dafoe Papers, J. W. Dafoe to Thomas Coté, Apr. 6, 1916.

[26]P.A.M., *Manitoba Debates*, (F.P.) 1916, p. 53.

[27]*Ibid.*, p. 48.

[28]*Ibid.*, p. 55.

University of Manitoba a state university, the year 1916 witnessed
the end of political controversy over the school question in the province of Manitoba.

V

The legislation of 1916 was enforced with both firmness and
tact[29]. But the Liberal party of Manitoba had to pay the penalty for
its courage in grasping the nettle. In 1920 it lost its majority to
candidates of the United Farmers and to opponents of the school legislation of 1916[30]. In 1922 its defeat was completed by the same forces.
The fusion of the United Farmers with the opponents of the school
legislation did not lead to any change in the school system. The
Liberal leader might argue that the combination was a revenge for
1916, but Premier John Bracken made it clear that no one had ever
suggested to him any change in the school system as the price of support.[31] Bracken's statement was never challenged in the debates. It
seems clear that once the personalities of 1916 were removed from
public office, the school question was a closed issue as far as the political
parties of Manitoba were concerned.   .

[29]P.A.M., Pamphlets, *Addresses in the Legislature by Hon. R. S. Thornton* 1917
to 1919. (Dept. of Education, Winnipeg, 1917, 1918, 1919. See also P.A.M.,
Manitoba Debates, (*F.P.*) 1921 pp. 83-89; *Ibid.,* 1917, 9; *Ibid.,* 1920, 30. I am
told on good authority that it was Dr. Thornton who coined the term, "New
Canadian".

[30]Dafoe Papers, J. W. Dafoe to Clifford Sifton, Dec. 29, 1920; *Canadian
Annual Review,* 1921, 739; *Manitoba Free Press,* Feb. 25, 1921, p. 13.

[31]The Farmers' Platform of 1922 merely called for stricter enforcement of
attendance, but made no reference to language instruction.

Church, Schools, and Politics in Manitoba, 1903-1912

RAMSAY COOK

ONE of the chief staples of political controversy during the Laurier administration was the problem of church-state relations, and more particularly the separate school question. Since Sir Wilfrid himself was a Roman Catholic and drew heavily on his native province for political support, he was an easy target for those who constituted themselves the guardians of English-Canadian Protestant virtue. They repeatedly charged him with undue susceptibility to clerical influence, despite the well-known fact that he and his party had openly opposed the demands of the Church hierarchy in settling the Manitoba school question in 1896. In 1905 the critics of the Liberal Government found opportunities on two separate occasions to accuse the administration of subservience to Roman Catholic wishes. The first occurred in connection with the autonomy bills and is well known to students of Canadian political history. A request from Manitoba for an extension of its boundaries provided the occasion for the second round of charges.

A representative of the Manitoba Government set the stage for the second controversy by charging that Sir Wilfrid in co-operation with the Apostolic Delegate, Mgr Sbaretti, was attempting to re-institute separate schools in Manitoba in return for extension of its boundaries. This incident deserves more attention than it has yet received for it provides some interesting illustrations of a number of the features of Canadian political history. First, it shows how far the Manitoba schools question was from being "settled" in 1896–7. At the same time it makes clear that despite the promptings and even threats of Mgr Sbaretti, Sir Wilfrid had no intention of deviating from the conciliatory stand he had taken on this question in 1896. Once again in these events Laurier the political craftsman is displayed to good advantage, explaining, temporizing, placating. Finally, the frictions between federal and provincial political parties can be studied against the background of a highly sensitive religious and racial question. By carrying the related events through to 1912, it is possible to show that Premier Borden was able to succeed in uniting

*The author would like to thank the Humanities Research Council and the Committee to administer the Rockefeller Grant at the University of Toronto for grants which made this study possible.

Reprinted from *Canadian Historical Review*, XXXIX (1), March, 1958

the interests of Dominion and provincial parties and to settle this thorny question after Sir Wilfrid had failed.

Though the subject of the school question as an issue in Manitoba politics has been investigated,[1] and the facts surrounding the boundary controversy recently set out,[2] very little attention has been paid to the rôle played by Mgr Sbaretti and the Manitoba Catholics in making the school question a constant irritant to Laurier and the Liberal party in Manitoba. Perhaps the subject has been somewhat overlooked because after 1905 it was never again allowed to erupt into federal politics during the Laurier term of office. Nevertheless the Manitoba school situation remained a problem of considerable political magnitude for Laurier and Borden, until the latter was able to work out an acceptable boundary settlement in 1912.[3]

The roots of the problem are found in the settlement of 1896. After Mgr Merry del Val's arrival in Canada in that year, the Papacy on his advice issued an encyclical instructing all Catholics to accept the Laurier-Greenway settlement. It was not to be looked upon as a final settlement, but rather as the only possibility in the circumstances, and a point of departure for future improvements. Thus from the Catholics' viewpoint the question was by no means settled, and therefore a potential source of future trouble. The arrival of a new Apostolic Delegate in 1902 heralded a new stage in the school controversy. Desiring to turn all his efforts to the well-being and prosperity of the Catholics of Canada, both from a spiritual and a temporal viewpoint, Mgr Sbaretti was not content to let the matter rest.[4]

In the spring of 1903 the Prime Minister supplied Mgr Sbaretti with a statement on the school situation as it then existed in Manitoba. He reviewed the question from its inception in the nineties, emphasizing the position taken by the bishops in Quebec in the 1896 election, in order to make clear the danger involved in allowing the question to become one of political controversy. He added that constant efforts were being made to settle the problem of the Winnipeg Catholics by bringing them under the city school board,

[1]W. L. Morton, "The Manitoba Schools and Canadian Nationalism, 1890–1916," *Canadian Historical Association Report, 1946,* 51–9.

[2]W. L. Morton, *Manitoba : A History* (Toronto, 1957), 273–329.

[3]O. D. Skelton, *Life and Letters of Sir Wilfrid Laurier* (2 vols., Toronto, 1921), II, 242; Morton, *Manitoba,* 292; R. Rumilly, *Histoire de la Province de Québec* (26 vols., Montreal, 1940–55), XII, 28. The charge made by Rogers is noted by each of these authors. The failure to give the question any detailed consideration is particularly curious in the case of Skelton whose biography was based on extensive use of the Laurier Papers.

[4]P.A.C., Laurier Papers, 246, Mgr Sbaretti to Laurier, Nov. 30, 1902.

thus releasing them from the burden of double taxation. Standing in the way of success, however, was one serious obstacle—Archbishop Langevin of St. Boniface. Laurier wrote:

Bien que Sa Grandeur soit douée d'un grand nombre des qualités très estimables, je ne crois pas qu'elle ait aucune de celles qui pourraient en faire un négociateur heureux. De plus, si je dois exprimer toute ma pensée, je suis convaincu que Sa Grandeur n'a jamais accepté de bonne grâce la législation de 1897, et n'a jamais sincèrement fait aucun effort pour la faire accepter à Winnipeg. Avec sa Grandeur, le résultat serait douteux; avec un autre, je serais certain du succès.[5]

Sir Wilfrid thus made his position clear; he was prepared to work for the betterment of the Catholic's position in Manitoba, but only through the method which he called "la politique de conciliation." But he was afraid that the greatest stumbling block to his conciliatory methods would be the doughty Archbishop of St. Boniface.

As a practical politician who believed that his "sunny ways" would ultimately achieve more for his Catholic fellow countrymen than uncompromising demands that excited racial and religious passions, Laurier naturally had little sympathy for a man of Archbishop Langevin's temperament. This western prelate fully subscribed to the Catholic belief in the necessity of denominational schools for the proper education of Catholic children.[6] But Archbishop Langevin was not merely a Catholic. Equally important was his French-Canadian origin, and he seems to have made little or no distinction between his religion and his nationality. He once warned his parishioners, "Sauver le français, c'est sauver une grande force catholique; l'anglais dans notre pays est une force pour l'hérésie."[7] Holding such views as these Mgr Langevin found little but frustration in Laurier's compromises.

During the spring of 1903 negotiations were set afoot in Winnipeg in an effort to settle the problem of the Catholic school children there. Laurier appealed to his supporters in Winnipeg to give their co-operation in bringing the matter to a successful conclusion, but although they were apparently willing to be of assistance, "the belief that Mr. Roblin has been working the thing up for supposedly political ends is the chief obstacle in the way of a peaceful settlement."[8] Here was really the crux of the problem in Manitoba: neither party trusted the other enough to attempt a settlement. The pawn

---

[5]*Ibid.*, 268, Laurier to Mgr Sbaretti, May 30, 1903.
[6]H. A. Rommen, *The State in Catholic Thought* (London, 1945), chap. xv.
[7]A. G. Morice, *Vie de Mgr Langevin* (St. Boniface, 1919), 383.
[8]Laurier Papers, 262, Laurier to J. W. Dafoe, April 26, 1903, and reply, May 2, 1903.

in this political game was the Catholic minority. When the negotiations in Winnipeg failed, all Sir Wilfrid could do after meeting a delegation of Catholics from Winnipeg was to appeal again to his Manitoba followers to make concessions.[9]

In the autumn of the same year the Apostolic Delegate himself visited Manitoba. He discussed the vexing school question with Premier Roblin and returned to Ottawa optimistic that a new settlement could be obtained provided the matter was kept on a non-partisan basis. Premier Roblin, so the Apostolic Delegate reported, was ready to open negotiations with Clifford Sifton and had indicated his willingness to enact any agreed changes "provided of course that the Government of Ottawa will be party in the arrangement." Though Sifton was absent in England the Prime Minister indicated his own willingness to give his "personal support to any measure that he [Roblin] will submit to the Legislature . . . and I will use my influence with my friends to the same end."[10]

Whether Sir Wilfrid ever asked Sifton to carry out this mission is not clear, but on finding that the substitution of Senator Dandurand was unacceptable to Mgr Sbaretti, he wrote personally to the Manitoba Premier. He made no commitment on his own behalf other than indicating his interest and concern in the matter, but he asked Roblin to inform him as to "the character and extent of the legislation which you contemplate." There was no offer of direct cooperation here and Roblin's refusal to "further consider the matter, at least for the moment" showed that he did not intend to venture out on a limb alone.[11] Nevertheless this approach represents Laurier's consistent position. He held that the responsibility for the school situation rested with the provincial authorities and though he would appeal to his followers to co-operate in any equitable solution, the federal government itself could not interfere in the matter.

This attitude did not win Mgr Sbaretti's approval. He was irritated because Laurier had not complied with his suggestion that Sifton be sent to negotiate with the Manitoba Government, and in writing to Premier Roblin the Apostolic Delegate felt that Sir Wilfrid had misrepresented the whole situation. As a result of his refusal to commit himself to any action, Laurier had probably let a golden opportunity for a settlement slip from his grasp.[12] In his letter to Roblin, Laurier had referred to a "new opening" in the school question, and this seriously alarmed the Catholic official:

[9]Ibid., 264, Laurier to J. W. Dafoe, Aug. 14, 1903.
[10]Ibid., 288, Mgr Sbaretti to Laurier, Oct. 29, 1903, and reply, Oct. 29, 1903.
[11]Ibid., 303, Laurier to R. P. Roblin, Jan. 27, 1904, and reply, Feb. 5, 1904.
[12]Ibid., Mgr Sbaretti to Laurier, Feb. 5, 1904.

In your letter there is mention of a *new opening* of the School Question. I really do not understand how a question which never was closed could be re-opened. I am obliged to say that neither the Catholics nor the hierarchy of Canada, nor the Holy See considered the question closed. And the fact that you yourself promised the Archbishops of Canada, my predecessor and myself, that the central Government would not give the school money and property to the Government of Manitoba until the question is settled to the satisfaction of the Catholics, shows that you considered the question being very far from closed.[13]

In his reply to this magisterial lecture the Prime Minister politely pointed out that "new opening" meant "new development," an explanation which Mgr Sbaretti accepted with ill grace.[14] It is noteworthy that Sir Wilfrid offered no denial of the promises referred to in the Papal Delegate's letter.

In March, 1904, Mgr Sbaretti began pressing for a statement of explicit guarantees for the rights of the minority in the Northwest Territories. After he had exacted from the Prime Minister the promise that the minority would not lose its school rights when the area was given provincial status he again turned to Manitoba.[15] His initial request was that as the *sine qua non* to the inclusion of any part of the Northwest Territories in Manitoba, the province should be obliged to maintain separate schools in the new territory. His objective however was made clear when he asked for a specific assurance that ". . . you will take the opportunity to settle the school question of Manitoba by exacting the re-establishment of the schools in return for the extension of the territory and the giving of the administration of the public lands."[16] This demand represents the core of the position that Mgr Sbaretti was to occupy during the remainder of his term in Canada. Laurier's answer was indefinite but it was obvious that he was not anxious to make any explicit statement on the question. He begged off by claiming that he had not had time to think the subject out "and for the present . . . would not undertake a binding engagement or even express a mature opinion."[17]

Temporizing was unsatisfactory to Mgr Sbaretti. He felt that Sir Wilfrid's repeated declarations that the school settlement could best be achieved through joint action on the federal and provincial levels meant that his own proposition should be acceptable. But the method, he said, was unimportant; the objective must take first

13*Ibid.*, Mgr Sbaretti to Laurier, Feb. 8, 1904.
14*Ibid.*, 304, Laurier to Mgr Sbaretti, Feb. 10, 1904, and reply, Feb. 11, 1904.
15*Ibid.*, 307, Laurier to Mgr Sbaretti, March 7, 1904.
16*Ibid.*, 312, Mgr Sbaretti to Laurier, April 7, 1904.
17*Ibid.*, Laurier to Mgr Sbaretti, April 11, 1904.

place. Still, if the Prime Minister did not have an alternative method to offer he felt it was desirable that the one suggested should be carefully considered and a definite agreement reached. Nevertheless Sir Wilfrid refused to be rushed.[18] He offered some encouragement to the Papal Delegate, though in doing so he only infuriated the churchman. He agreed that if any portion of the Northwest Territories where separate schools existed was transferred to Manitoba, these schools would be protected. But even this concession he qualified by stating that if the territory contained no Catholics and no existing separate schools "the case would present another aspect and would suggest a different conclusion."[19]

The two men now entered a difficult phase of their debate and signs of serious strain began to appear. The Papal Delegate, a man with a single cause at heart, pressed his argument with all the logic of the schools in which he had been trained and sometimes in language which suggests that diplomacy was not his strongest characteristic. He was understandably exasperated by the Prime Minister who, in his awareness that Manitoba Roman Catholics were not the only interest group he had to satisfy, would sometimes seem to accept all the premises of an argument yet still ignore the most obvious conclusion. The suggestion that there might not be any Catholic in the territories seemed totally irrelevant to Mgr Sbaretti; there was a principle at stake which could not be measured in numbers. Furthermore there was the future to consider, a future which might see a large-scale influx of Roman Catholics into the territory.[20] Laurier's methods, evolved in an awareness of the limitations of logic in the governance of men, could only be anathema to one completely convinced of the righteousness of his cause. Sir Wilfrid wrote on one occasion: "I recognize the force and logic of your argument. Still I would like to reserve judgment for further consideration, as the result of all experience in constitutional government has demonstrated that a close adherence to logic may lead into practical difficulties. Let me add that before coming to any definite conclusion, I will again discuss the matter with Your Excellency."[21]

The church official's reaction showed a complete lack of sympathy with Laurier's difficulties. "Practical difficulties" to the Premier were those involved in governing a country divided on racial and religious lines. The only difficulties recognized by Mgr Sbaretti were those of

---

[18]*Ibid.*, Mgr Sbaretti to Laurier, April 13, 1904, and reply, April 16, 1904.
[19]*Ibid.*, Laurier to Mgr Sbaretti, April 22, 1904.
[20]*Ibid.*, Mgr Sbaretti to Laurier, April 24, 1904.
[21]*Ibid.*, Laurier to Mgr Sbaretti, May 4, 1904.

Catholics who had been deprived of their separate schools. It was obvious to the clear, analytical mind of the man trained in exegetical exercises that "practical difficulties are not created by a law establishing Separate Schools, but were and are created by the want or abrogation of such a law."[22]

Here, for the moment, the debate rested. Clearly no common ground had been established. While the Papal Delegate quite naturally considered the problem strictly from the viewpoint of his Church, Laurier, though interested in promoting the cause of justice for his fellow Catholics, was convinced that a political decision required a careful balancing of a variety of forces. To him the matter was far more complex than Mgr Sbaretti was prepared to recognize. For reasons of constitutional propriety and political expediency, direct federal interference in Manitoba educational arrangements was impossible.

The decision of the Laurier Government in 1905 to give provincial status to the Northwest Territories naturally stimulated Manitoba's desire to fulfil her manifest northward destiny. At the same time the announcement that the Manitoba legislature had unanimously resolved in favour of boundary extension again brought the school question sharply to the Apostolic Delegate's attention. Fresh from successfully obtaining from the Government certain guarantees respecting minority rights in the new provinces, he now felt the moment to be propitious for a similar agreement to cover any territorial grants made to Manitoba.[23] His attitude had not softened in any way, and he still refused to consider the question in relation to the Government's political position. His proposal was blunt:

It is my conviction that the actual demand of Manitoba offers an opportunity to settle the School Question in that Province to the satisfaction of Catholics. What the Province asks is within the jurisdiction of the Dominion Parliament. The Dominion Parliament is not obliged to cede the territory, the Dominion Government can use such a demand as a lever to bring Manitoba to ameliorate the position of the Catholics in the Province—much more, since the Roblin Government claims to be friendly to the Catholics of the Province, this would afford an opportunity of proving its friendliness.[24]

To this maximum demand he added what was apparently an acceptable minimum. If the suggested bargain proved unacceptable, at least the existing separate schools could be preserved by inserting

22Ibid., Mgr Sbaretti to Laurier, May 6, 1904.
23Ibid., 246, Mgr Sbaretti to Laurier, March 1, 1904, and reply, March 7, 1904; ibid., 359, Mgr Sbaretti to Laurier, March 13, 1905.
24Ibid., 352, Mgr Sbaretti to Laurier, Jan. 21, 1905.

in the legislation providing for transfer a clause prohibiting the application of the Manitoba School Act in the new territory. The Prime Minister made no commitment to either proposition. He answered briefly that his desire for a short session of Parliament coupled with the large amount of necessary business already on the agenda would make it impossible to deal with the Manitoba request.[25] When the Manitoba delegates arrived in Ottawa Mgr Sbaretti again wrote to Sir Wilfrid asking him if he could not at least "insinuate to these delegates that an amelioration of the condition of the Catholics in Manitoba with regard to the schools would remove difficulties."[26] The Prime Minister apparently made no written reply to this suggestion, but he certainly did not adopt it.

In the meantime the Canadian House of Commons was turning its attention to the autonomy bills. Already the charge that the educational provisions for the new provincial constitutions had been shaped by Mgr Sbaretti was being aired.[27] Laurier was entering upon one of the most serious crises of his political career and it is inconceivable that he should have created further difficulties for himself by reopening the Manitoba school issue. There were others, however, not adverse to increasing the Premier's difficulties. Among these was Robert Rogers, a member of the Manitoba Government visiting Ottawa for the purpose of forwarding his province's boundary extension case. Rogers apparently felt that the federal government had more reasons than those made public for refusing the provincial request for territorial expansion. He had some further reasons to offer, and the fact that these reasons appeared to substantiate the charges that his fellow Conservatives were making about the relations between Laurier and Mgr Sbaretti only made them more convincing. So Rogers unburdened himself of a lengthy statement which appeared in the *Ottawa Citizen* and other eastern papers on April 4, and provided material for debate in the House of Commons on the two following days.

The substance of Rogers' charge was that while he and his colleague, Colin Campbell, were waiting in Ottawa for Laurier's answer to the proposal for boundary changes they had been called into conference by the Papal Delegate. The latter presented them with an outline of certain changes which the Roman Catholic Church desired to have made in the Manitoba School Act. He then

[25]*Ibid.*, Laurier to Mgr Sbaretti, Feb. 17, 1905.
[26]*Ibid.*, 355, Mgr Sbaretti to Laurier, Feb. 17, 1905.
[27]Canada, House of Commons, *Debates*, 1905, II, 4010; *Canadian Annual Review*, 1905, 71–4.

implied that if these requests were accepted, boundary extension would be expedited.[28] To Rogers the meaning of this request was obvious:

What more natural conclusion can be arrived at than that Sir Wilfrid is simply killing time and making pretexts in order that the polite invitation of Mgr. Sbaretti could be acted upon by Manitoba?

In this way of course, Sir Wilfrid thinks he can secure a political advantage for his friends in this province. This is a palpable political trick, which he is quite capable of undertaking with a view to forcing the local government to do something which would be resented by the people and by this means he hopes to reinstate his Liberal friends in power here. . . . I deny the right of Sir Wilfrid and Monseigneur Sbaretti to mix up the matter of separate schools with that of extension of our boundaries, and I am sure that in doing so they do not reflect the wishes of either the Roman Catholics or the Protestants in the Province. . . .[29]

Rogers had more to add to the indictment, for as a skilful politician he was aware of the use that could be made of this issue in Manitoba political warfare.[30] He documented his charges by reaching back to the school controversy of 1896 and the negotiations which brought Mgr Merry del Val to Canada. He cited a letter in which Charles Russell, the Canadian government's legal representative in London, had pointed out to the authorities at Rome regarding the Laurier-Greenway settlement: "We do not solicit His Holiness to sanction as perfect the concessions obtained, but that in his wisdom he will be pleased to regard them as the beginning of justice." What other conclusion was possible but that the scheme set afoot by Laurier and Mgr del Val in 1896 was now to be carried to its conclusion by Laurier and Mgr Sbaretti?[31]

Naturally the Conservative Opposition found such sensational claims by an influential member of the Manitoba Conservative Government convincing proof of a Laurier-Sbaretti conspiracy. The *Hamilton Spectator* called Laurier "a puppet in the hands of a foreign Dignitary who makes and unmakes Provinces as he pleases."[32] The Government's critics were also able to adduce other evidence to support Rogers' charges. They pointed out that the *North West Review*, the journal of the English-speaking Catholics in Manitoba, and *Le Soleil*, an avowed organ of the Liberals in Quebec, had both argued that so long as Manitoba maintained its iniquitous school

[28]Canada, House of Commons, *Debates*, 1905, II, 3835.

[29]*Ibid.* That Robert Rogers was using this information in a by-election campaign is no doubt worth mention (Morton, *Manitoba*, 292).

[30]Morton, "The Manitoba Schools and Canadian Nationalism," 51–9.

[31]Canada, House of Commons, *Debates*, 1905, II, 3837.

[32]*Canadian Annual Review*, 1905, 97.

legislation it would deservedly remain the smallest western province.[33]

Here certainly was grape-shot for a full-scale Opposition broadside on the Government's entire record on the Manitoba schools and more especially on its relations with the Roman Catholic Church. The chief contention was that the Papal Delegate had been sent to Canada in answer to a petition from the Laurier Government. His purpose, as W. F. MacLean put it, was to act as "an appanage of the Grit machine . . . the policeman with the big stick to discipline the Bishops and the clergy of the Roman Catholic Church. . . ." Since in interfering with matters of politics and government he had overstepped his jurisdiction, the Government must take the responsibility and have him recalled as it had had Lord Dundonald recalled.[34] This was a charge that stung.

Laurier's reply was that the charge of collusion between the Papal Delegate and himself had not "a shadow or tittle of truth in it." Furthermore he denied that his Government had invited the Apostolic Delegate to Canada in 1896: he had come on the invitation of a number of Roman Catholics, some of whom were members of the Government, to settle some difficulties that had arisen in the Roman Catholic Church, and not for any political purpose.[35]

Mgr Sbaretti was equally categorical in his denial of the charges made by "Bob" Rogers, or at least of the implications that had been drawn. In a public statement issued on April 6, he admitted having had an interview with Colin Campbell, the Manitoba Attorney General, but denied that the second minister was present. The subject of the discussion had been the Manitoba School Act, particularly its effect on Catholics in Winnipeg and Brandon. He admitted that he had suggested certain changes to remedy the situation that the Catholics in these centres found themselves in. He continued:

I urged my request on the ground of fairness and justice and, referring to the object of his mission to Ottawa, I remarked from the point of view of the Manitoba Government some action on these lines would be politically expedient and tend to facilitate the accomplishment of his object; inasmuch as Catholics in any territory which might be annexed to Manitoba would naturally object to losing the right to Separate Schools and to be subjected to the educational conditions which existed in Manitoba. . . .

The Federal Government had absolutely no knowledge of it. It was a private conversation and simply intended to express a suggestion and a desire that the

[33]Canada, House of Commons, *Debates*, 1905, II, 3940 and 3942.
[34]*Ibid.*, 3863–986.
[35]*Ibid.*, 3837–46.

condition of the Catholics in the respects mentioned should be improved. Any other assumption or interpretation is altogether unfounded. . . .[36]

In the face of these denials it appeared that the Manitoba Minister had laboured mightily and brought forth a mouse. The members of the federal Opposition, with the fruitful field of the autonomy bills still stretching before them, dropped the Manitoba incident. In Manitoba, however, Premier Roblin's supporters continued to claim that Laurier's ambition was to force separate schools on the province until the day the Liberal Government left office.[37]

Thus the evidence supports the conclusion that Rogers' charge in 1905 was baseless. Laurier had at no time encouraged the Papal Delegate in his belief that the proposed boundary extension afforded an opportunity to gain school concessions for the Catholics in Manitoba. In fact, as he had informed Mgr Sbaretti, he was not even prepared to consider the Manitoba boundary question in 1905. He explained to the House of Commons that Quebec, Ontario, and Saskatchewan were interested in the territory requested by Manitoba and they would have to be consulted.[38] That there was need for consultation is made evident by the fact that one Ontario member of the Laurier Government, Postmaster General Mulock, had made known his opposition to any division of territory that denied Ontario a port on Hudson Bay.[39] Thus the claim of Premier Roblin's biographer that the "circumstantial evidence" indicates that Laurier "would have made good Sbaretti's implied promise"[40] does not conform to the evidence. In discussing the matter with Mgr Sbaretti Laurier went no further than to agree to consider the suggestion, while at the same time offering strong objections to it. At no time did he hold out any hope that he would follow the Papal Delegate's suggestions, but rather discouraged this belief. There was justice in the exclamation of the Manitoba Liberal editor who wrote: "The Rogers' manifesto was as deliberate an attempt to dupe and gull the public as was ever played by a card-sharper or thimble rigger at a fair."[41]

The controversy which resulted from his intervention in the

[36]*Canadian Annual Review*, 1905, 95–6.

[37]Laurier Papers, 648, Laurier to J. W. Dafoe, Oct. 25, 1910; *Manitoba Free Press*, June 21, 1911.

[38]Canada, House of Commons, *Debates*, 1905, I, 1429–31.

[39]Ontario, Public Archives, Whitney Papers, R. L. Borden to James Whitney, April 27, 1905.

[40]H. R. Ross, *Thirty-five Years in the Limelight: Sir Rodmond P. Roblin and His Times* (Winnipeg, 1936), 126.

[41]*Manitoba Free Press*, April 7, 1908.

Manitoba boundary negotiations did not weaken Mgr Sbaretti's
determination to press for the redress of Catholic educational grievances in Manitoba. The Papal Delegate knew his duty well and
intended to pursue the school question with the persistence that
was now all too familiar to Sir Wilfrid. Early in 1906 Mgr Sbaretti
began new negotiations with school officials in Winnipeg. He soon
appealed to Sir Wilfrid for help, claiming that "The Free Press and
the Liberal party are trying to make political capital" out of the
school question.[42] Laurier immediately wrote to the newspaper's
editor asking him "not to allow another school question to develop
in Manitoba," and appealing for his assistance in the negotiations
which were then in progress. The reply from Winnipeg gave little
hope for success. Lack of confidence in Premier Roblin and Archbishop Langevin made the Manitoba Liberals reluctant to show
their hand in the politically explosive educational question.[43] The
negotiations failed.

In November, 1906, a conference was called in Ottawa among the
governments interested in the disposition of the territory of Keewatin. Preparatory to the conference Laurier had consulted his Manitoba supporters, but they apparently had been unable to decide
whether boundary extension would aid or deter the party interest in
the province.[44] As the Apostolic Delegate was visiting Rome when
the proposed conference was announced, his secretary wrote to
remind Laurier of the Church's interest in the proceedings.[45] On
the day the conference opened, Mgr Sbaretti informed Laurier that
Cardinal Merry del Val and the authorities at Rome felt that the
boundary negotiations offered an excellent opportunity to reopen
the school question.[46]

The conference had ended in disagreement over the territorial
division before Laurier was able to find time to reply to the prelate.
He now took the occasion to make explicit his views on the problems
arising from Manitoba's territorial ambitions. The school question,
he said, must be recognized as taking secondary place to the primary
consideration which was Manitoba's just claim to a large portion of
the territory of Keewatin. To attach any conditions to the transfer of
these lands to Manitoba would at once place the minority in "a very
invidious position," the position of opposing the almost unamimous

[42]Laurier Papers, 402, Mgr Sbaretti to Laurier, Feb. 21, 1906.
[43]Ibid., 404, Laurier to J. W. Dafoe, Feb. 28, 1906, and reply, March 19, 1906.
[44]Ibid., 435, Laurier to E. Brown, Nov. 14, 1906.
[45]Ibid., 430, Rev. Alfred Sinnott to Laurier, Oct. 20, 1906.
[46]Ibid., 435, Mgr Sbaretti to Laurier, Nov. 11, 1906.

will of Manitoba. The existing school laws must apply to any new territory acquired by the province. Finally, he denied that the annexation of Keewatin to the Northwest Territories in 1905 had any bearing on the school question. This temporary arrangement had been made by his government for strictly administrative purposes.[47] Mgr Sbaretti was unconvinced. He insisted that the attachment of Keewatin to the Northwest Territories brought the former area under the school laws of the territories which provided for separate schools. The Premier saw immediately that the adoption of this view would be an invitation to disaster. His critics would eagerly grasp the opportunity to attack him for having "purposely delayed the consideration of Manitoba's application for the purpose of altering the conditions then existing, and forcing upon Manitoba a restriction as to its power of legislation in matters of education."[48] Such evident duplicity would make his continuance in office impossible and abruptly end his usefulness to the Roman Catholics in Canada. In short Sir Wilfrid had decided that the school question could not be allowed to complicate the boundary extension negotiations. The door to further discussion remained ajar, as always, but the Premier's conviction was firm and unshakable. In this microcosmic conflict of empire and papacy, Sir Wilfrid was determined not to travel to Canossa.

In Manitoba as long as the boundary question remained unsettled the Roblin Government faced an Opposition that was seriously handicapped. Though it has been suggested that Laurier refused to offer Manitoba acceptable terms for boundary extension because his provincial allies did not want Roblin to obtain credit for the settlement,[49] the fact is that by 1907 the Manitoba Liberals wanted the question settled. They were finally convinced that a generous agreement would benefit their cause, if only by removing the matter from the realm of controversy.[50] Laurier was not to be rushed, however, and expressed the hope to the provincial party leader "that you will agree with me that there is no hurry" for a settlement.[51]

Whether the Prime Minister was temporizing because of the continued insistence of the Papal Delegate's demands is impossible to ascertain, but Mgr Sbaretti was certainly far from convinced that Manitoba could not be forced to modify its school laws. He

[47]Ibid., 438, Laurier to Mgr Sbaretti, Dec. 10, 1906.
[48]Ibid., 443, Mgr Sbaretti to Laurier, Jan. 15, 1907, and reply, Feb. 2, 1907.
[49]Ross, Roblin, 119.
[50]Laurier Papers, 450, J. W. Dafoe to Laurier, Jan. 7, 1907; ibid., Rev. Geo. Bryce to Laurier, Feb. 22, 1907; ibid., 442, E. Brown to Laurier, Jan. 7, 1907.
[51]Ibid., 442, Laurier to E. Brown, Jan. 11, 1907.

refused to retreat from the position that it was the duty of the Laurier Government "to guarantee the said rights and I do not see how the Federal Government can fail to accomplish these obligations toward the minority, . . ."[52]

In June, 1907, Laurier visited Mgr Sbaretti in Rome, but the changed surroundings failed to alter the views of either party.[53] Back in Ottawa in the autumn, however, the discussion moved on to a new level. Mgr Sbaretti was now temporarily willing to drop the discussion of abstract rights and duties, and to explore political considerations. This was the heart of the matter. The prelate argued that Sir Wilfrid's prestige would easily extinguish the sparks of opposition that would be generated if Manitoba were forced to modify her school laws. Similar sparks in 1905 had been prevented from bursting into a general conflagration. That Mgr Sbaretti's ability to estimate the combustibility of the school issue was limited by his zeal to win justice for the members of his church was evident from a new plan he put forward to protect the Keewatin Catholics. Since the school laws in Saskatchewan and Ontario were favourable to the minority, Keewatin should be divided between these two provinces and the boundaries of Manitoba left unchanged.[54]

Sir Wilfrid knew that such a solution was unjust and impossible. Manitoba's right to the territory on its northern boundary was unquestionable. In a revealing reply Laurier offered an assessment of his strength and a statement of his first duty:

I have already, and at some length, given you the reasons which in my humble judgment render such action absolutely impossible. In our conversation last Sunday evening I again repeated them, and I must once more express my conviction that not only do I not think that even with the authority which I may have in the House, I could carry such a measure, but to attempt it would rouse such an agitation as would prove most dangerous to the welfare of this community. It was evident to me last Sunday that on this point I failed to convince Your Excellency. Your letter now makes this very plain.[55]

The futile reiteration of arguments seemed to be growing tiresome to Sir Wilfrid. He wished to conclude the discussion. The school question was completely divorced from the boundaries and must be regarded as a separate issue. Now he would not even consider renewed negotiations with the Manitoba Government for he was convinced that "even with no opposition facing him, Mr. Roblin

[52]Ibid., 451, Mgr Sbaretti to Laurier, Jan. 11, 1907.
[53]Ibid., 465, Laurier to Mgr Sbaretti, June 1, 1907.
[54]Ibid., 475, Mgr. Sbaretti to Laurier, Aug. 27, 1907.
[55]Ibid., Laurier to Mgr Sbaretti, Aug. 28, 1907.

would not undertake the task because opposition from within his party would crush him."[56]

Yet Sir Wilfrid probably knew Mgr Sbaretti well enough to realize that this lengthy and completely unambiguous statement would not be convincing. The Speech from the Throne in December announced that Manitoba would be offered expanded boundaries. Before the House of Commons debated the question, Laurier informed the Papal Delegate that no limitation on Manitoba's jurisdiction over education was to be included in the proposed resolution. Mgr Sbaretti's reaction was one of "extreme displeasure."[57] When R. W. Scott, one of Laurier's Catholic colleagues, urged the Papal Delegate to accept the Prime Minister's view, he received an equally peremptory reply stating that the difference between the Government and the Church arose from judging the question by "a different criterion." He was left in no doubt as to which was the correct criterion.[58]

The Government had settled on its policy. Although the weight of the Archbishop of Toronto was added in support of Mgr Sbaretti's opinion,[59] the Minister of Justice was instructed to prepare a resolution regarding the boundary extension which made no mention of the school question.[60] It is interesting to note that there was apprehension and suspicion in Manitoba Liberal circles about the intentions of the Prime Minister in the boundary matter. J. W. Dafoe, no doubt recalling the 1905 troubles, felt that the enigmatic Sir Wilfrid should be impressed with the extreme danger of attempting to force educational changes on Manitoba as part of a boundary extension deal. "It is impossible to see just what would happen should any such colossal blunder be made, but it would be an unrelieved disaster for Liberalism," he warned.[61]

The resolution setting out the terms offered to Manitoba for boundary extension, which left the financial terms unspecified, passed the House of Commons in July, 1908.[62] No further action resulted, however, since Manitoba was not satisfied with the terms offered, although Premier Whitney thought that the territorial offer to Manitoba was generous.[63] The Roblin Government's demand for

[56]Ibid.
[57]Ibid., 495, Laurier to Mgr Sbaretti, Dec. 16, 1907, and reply, Dec. 16, 1907.
[58]Ibid., 496, R. W. Scott to Mgr Sbaretti, Dec. 30, 1907; P.A.C., R. W. Scott Papers, 1, Mgr Sbaretti to R. W. Scott, Jan. 3, 1908.
[59]Laurier Papers, 505, Archbishop McEvay to Laurier, Feb. 17, 1908.
[60]Ibid., 521, Laurier to A. B. Aylesworth, June 11, 1908.
[61]P.A.C., Sifton Papers, J. W. Dafoe to Sir Clifford Sifton, July 7, 1908.
[62]Canada, House of Commons, Debates, 1907–8, VII, 12822.
[63]Whitney Papers, James Whitney to Robert Rogers, July 16, 1908.

financial "equality" with the other western provinces was unacceptable to Ottawa.[64]

Despite this failure Laurier decided early in 1909 to move from
resolution to definite legislation in the Manitoba dispute. This was
the cue for the Papal Delegate to make a new entrance. Negotiations
were again afoot with the Manitoba Government and he requested
more time. His mood was imperious: "If my hope is realized it may
be subject to the reasonable condition that these amendments be
asked for by you, and I do not see how you could possibly refuse to
make a request which would be granted."[65]

A distinct note of irritation now appeared in Laurier's attitude
to the indomitable churchman's demands. In the first place the
Prime Minister thoroughly distrusted Premier Roblin who was reported to have charged in a recent speech that Laurier intended to
force Manitoba to re-establish separate schools.[66] Such demagoguery
destroyed all hope for a negotiated agreement. What really stirred
his anger, however, was Mgr Sbaretti's threat that if the Liberal
Government did not meet the Church's requests, it would be "denounced" by Catholics. Laurier obviously resented the suggestion
that he could be coerced: "The expression 'the Catholics' is rather
vague, and I do not know exactly what it means, but without
probing it in any way let me assure Your Excellency, that if my co-
religionists withdraw from me the support with which they have
hitherto honoured me, I will be quite ready to accept the defeat of
the Government and to hand over to Mr. Borden the responsibility
of administering this country."[67]

It is probable that Sir Wilfrid felt some relief when Mgr Sbaretti
left Canada early in 1910. Certainly the Prime Minister's stoic
patience had been stretched almost to the limit at times in the
years of dispute over the Manitoba school question. The reminders
that he received during the closing period of the Liberal administration of the Church's continued interest in the Manitoba minority
were indeed mild compared with Mgr Sbaretti's impatient
demands.[68]

Though Mgr Sbaretti had spoken to Laurier on behalf of all the
Manitoba Catholics, this group was not in fact a united family.

[64]*Canada, Sessional Papers*, no. 110a. For a critical analysis of the financial aspect of the whole question see J. W. Maxwell, *Federal Subsidies to Provincial Governments* (Cambridge, 1923), 128 ff.

[65]Laurier Papers, 560, Mgr Sbaretti to Laurier, Feb. 14, 1909.

[66]*Ibid.*, 554, D. A. Ross to Laurier, Jan. 11, 1909.

[67]*Ibid.*, 560, Laurier to Mgr Sbaretti, Feb. 16, 1909.

[68]*Ibid.*, 650, Rev. Alfred Sinnott to Laurier, Nov. 14, 1910, and reply, Nov. 15, 1910.

Between the English-speaking Catholics in Manitoba and the hierarchy led by Mgr Langevin, there was little filial attachment. Many of the English Catholics felt that their failure to be released from the burden of double school taxation was chiefly due to the intransigence and impolitic behaviour of the St. Boniface Archbishop. In 1905 one group of non-French Catholics had publicly disapproved of their Archbishop's views on school policy.[69] This was a heresy which Mgr Langevin explained by the fact that the Irish Catholics were English speaking.[70] In the spring of 1909 when Laurier and Mgr Sbaretti were in the midst of their controversy, a leader of the Irish Catholic community in Winnipeg interviewed the Papal Delegate in an effort to explain the difficulties of the Catholic Church in Manitoba. Though Laurier was fully informed of the substance of the interview he probably had no part in initiating the mission. The chief complaint was that the Archbishop, who was regarded as the Catholic spokesman by Protestant Manitoba, was injuring the Church's cause in pressing extreme demands. Further harm was done by the fact that the St. Boniface prelate had allied himself to the Roblin Government because of an abiding distrust and even hatred of Sir Wilfrid. A simple, but far-reaching, solution was proposed: "I have pointed out to Your Excellency the necessity of appointing an English speaking Bishop in Winnipeg. Let us have a wise, prudent and conciliatory Churchman in Winnipeg and I confidently believe that the school trouble will be a thing of the past. Peace and harmony will reign where discord and bigotry now exist."[71] Finally he warned against supporting the suggestion of the Archbishop that the boundary extension plan offered an opportunity to exact school concessions from the Manitoba Government. Public opinion in Manitoba would never agree to such a proposal. Whatever Mgr Sbaretti may have thought of this outspoken criticism of his Manitoba colleague, the proposed change in the hierarchy was not approved.

During the autumn of 1910 Laurier visited the West to feel the political pulse of the embattled prairie farmer. In Winnipeg a delegation of English-speaking Catholics asked him to approach the Roblin Government on their behalf. Sir Wilfrid's reply was that there had been no new indication that the provincial government was prepared to offer any solution to the school difficulties. On the contrary the question had been constantly treated as a political football in a game with rules so arbitrary that he dared not par-

[69]Rumilly, *Histoire*, XII, 44.
[70]Morice, *Mgr Langevin*, 275.
[71]Laurier Papers, 563, J. K. Barrett to Mgr Sbaretti, Feb. 28, 1909.

ticipate in it.[72] Later in the year a representative of the same group reported to Laurier that, "The English speaking Catholics have thrown Archbishop Langevin, bag and baggage, overboard and have taken all their interests into their own hands." The Archbishop was accused of propagating the gospel according to Bourassa in Manitoba. In complete disgust, the English Catholics had devised a new approach to the school question. The plan was to form a bi-partisan committee to interview the Manitoba party leaders. Their offer would be to accept the Manitoba School Act, including a compulsory attendance clause, provided they were allowed to have Catholic teachers in their schools. Laurier was asked to obtain the support of his friends in the province in carrying out the plan.[73] The President of the Manitoba Liberal Association, who was aware of the English Catholics' plan, offered little hope of success. Since it was impossible to place any faith in the Roblin Government he could not see "how the Liberals in the House could make any arrangement before the concrete proposition was placed before them."[74] On the rocks of suspicion the new plan was wrecked.

The frustrations of the non-French Catholics in Manitoba apparently reached such a peak by the end of 1910 that they felt it necessary to make another appeal to higher authority. Since no successor had been appointed to replace Mgr Sbaretti in Canada, a delegate of the Irish Catholics in Winnipeg journeyed to Washington to place their case before the Apostolic Delegate to the United States, Mgr Falconio. The Archbishop of St. Boniface and his priests, Mgr Falconio was told, were undermining the welfare of the Church in Manitoba by espousing the cause of French-Canadian nationalism. The indictment was severe:

Can Your Excellency realize what this means for the Church? While assiduously labouring to maintain this narrow nationalism in which Christ and his Church hold only a nominal priority, the Catholics in all other races are neglected and ignored. The whole national movement of which the Archbishop of St. Boniface is a leader, is not concerned in the interests of religion but is its deadly enemy. Two strong factors are its controlling motives—namely, political and national domination, and the Archbishop of St. Boniface is a past master in both these objects.[75]

A request was made for the immediate despatch of a new Apostolic Delegate to Canada to avoid "anarchy and schism." Clearly the Roman Catholic Church was not the monolithic edifice that many

[72]*Ibid.*, Winnipeg Delegation Re: Separate Schools, Sept. 4, 1910.
[73]*Ibid.*, 654, J. K. Barrette to Laurier, Dec. 2, 1910. At the Eucharistic Conference in September, 1910, Mgr Langevin characterized as "le grand blessé de l'Ouest," had definitely identified himself with Henri Bourassa. (Rumilly, *Histoire*, XV, 111.)
[74]Laurier Papers, 658, Frank Fowler to Laurier, Dec. 30. 1910.
[75]*Ibid.*, 668, J. K. Barrette to The Most Reverend D. Falconio, March 1, 1911.

Protestants believed. It too had its divisions, and in Manitoba it was a bitter division.

When the campaigning for the 1911 election began, none of these questions which troubled the waters of Manitoba political and religious life had been settled. Manitoba remained the "postage stamp province"; the Winnipeg Catholics had obtained no relief from their burdensome tax load; Archbishop Langevin still reigned at St. Boniface. The events of the 1911 reciprocity election are well known. Manitoba returned eight supporters for the new Borden Government, a fact which caused Sir Wilfrid to comment bitterly: "Manitoba does not disappoint me because it is always the same in that province. It always shouts one way and votes the other."[76] This rancorous remark was not entirely justified. True, Manitoba farmers had "shouted" in chorus with other western farmers for a lower tariff, but the general treatment of Manitoba by the Liberal administration was not beyond reproach. The one large question which the Liberals had failed to answer was that concerning the boundaries. These remained unextended, and some Manitobans no doubt suspected that this fact was somehow connected with the ever present school question. It was only natural that in the election campaign the Conservatives, fearing the unpopularity of their stand on the trade question, should attempt to turn the minds of voters to issues on which the Liberals were more vulnerable. Mr. Borden, on his western tour during the spring recess of 1911, devoted at least one full speech in Manitoba to the boundary question. He promised a generous settlement if Manitobans gave him their support.[77] That it continued to be an issue throughout the campaign is suggested by the editorial page of the *Manitoba Free Press*. Although this Liberal journal attempted to keep attention focused on reciprocity, on several occasions it had to grapple with local Conservatives who were attempting to cloud the issue by introducing the boundary question.[78] It cannot be claimed that the boundary dispute was of primary importance in the 1911 election in Manitoba, but certainly it was a secondary issue capable of influencing doubtful voters. Manitobans had in the boundary question a legitimate grievance which the Liberals had been unable to redress. Sir Wilfrid had successfully staved off the demands of Mgr Sbaretti only to be outmanœuvred by the Roblin-Rogers combination.

[76]*Ibid.*, 691, Laurier to Dr. J. H. King, Sept. 23, 1911.
[77]*Manitoba Free Press*, June 21, 1911.
[78]*Ibid.*, Aug. 22, 1911 and Sept. 1, 1911. See also speech by Laurier, in Canada, House of Commons, *Debates*, 1911–12, 111, 4359, in which he states that the Conservatives emphasized the boundary question in the 1911 election campaign in Manitoba.

It now remained for the new Conservative Government to pre-
scribe a cure for the inferiority complex suffered by the diminutive
western province. The new Government was soon made sharply
aware of the pressures which had caused its predecessor to stumble
in attempting to settle the boundary question. Indeed the composition of Borden's cabinet and party made the Keewatin problem
an early test of the freshman Prime Minister's political skill. Two
members of the cabinet, Frank Cochrane of Ontario and Robert
Rogers of Manitoba, had come directly from the provincial cabinets
most concerned about the territorial division. Prime Minister Borden
owed a considerable debt of gratitude to the premiers of both these
provinces for the position he now held, and could not afford to
disappoint either of them. A consideration of no less importance
was the fact that his Quebec supporters led by F. D. Monk, but
inspired by the Nationalist promptings of Henri Bourassa, were
keenly sensitive to the claims of the Catholic minority in Keewatin.[79]

The haste with which Premier Roblin despatched his emissaries to
Ottawa after the election to discuss boundary extension caused
Premier Whitney some consternation.[80] The Ontario Premier's position was awkward. He felt that Premier Roblin was breaking faith
with him in pressing the federal authorities to settle the question
without first consulting Ontario. He had reason to be disgruntled,
for under the Laurier régime he had agreed to a request from Robert
Rogers to refrain from pressing for a settlement because Manitoba
felt the time inopportune.[81] His objective now was the same as it
had been earlier—the port on Hudson Bay which the 1908 resolution
had denied Ontario. In an election year it was important that this
concession be granted as the local Liberal Opposition was asking
embarrassing questions. The Ontario Premier was no amateur in the
game of politics, and knew how to bargain for what he wanted:

> You know very well that Ontario is not looking for territory [he told Frank
> Cochrane], and we are willing to do almost anything to avoid trouble and get
> a port. The matter has now arrived at such a stage that our political opponents
> accuse us of neglecting our duty, and although I shall be sorry to do so, yet if
> necessary I shall feel compelled to call on every one of the seventy-two
> government supporters from Ontario to take an active and individual part in
> assisting us in this matter.[82]

[79]See Heath Macquarrie, "The Formation of Borden's First Cabinet," *Canadian Journal of Economics and Political Science*, XXIII (Feb., 1957), 90–104, for an excellent discussion of the groups represented in Borden's cabinet.
[80]Whitney Papers, James Whitney to Frank Cochrane, Nov. 17, 1911.
[81]*Ibid.*, James Whitney to Sir Lomer Gouin, Dec. 30, 1910, and James Whitney to Frank Cochrane, Dec. 14, 1911.
[82]*Ibid.*, James Whitney to Frank Cochrane, Jan. 12, 1912, and James Whitney to R. L. Borden, Jan. 18, 1912.

Whitney was further disconcerted by the apparently unfounded claim of Robert Rogers, in November, 1911, that the question was settled. This bombshell burst right in the midst of the Ontario provincial election contest.[83] Borden knew that Whitney as well as Roblin had to be given satisfaction. Lengthy negotiations between Ottawa and Queen's Park resulted in a neat compromise which gave Ontario a right-of-way to build a railway to the ports of Churchill and Nelson in Manitoba territory.[84]

Thus two of the interested parties had been appeased, but the third, the Keewatin minority and its parliamentary spokesmen, presented a more difficult problem. Mgr Langevin petitioned Borden to safeguard Catholic schools in Keewatin so that these rights would not be lost when Manitoba acquired the territory.[85] Bishop Charlebois of Keewatin made a similar plea, but the Prime Minister made no commitments.[86]

The legislation providing for the territorial transfer came down to the House of Commons in February, 1912. Like Laurier's 1908 resolution it omitted any reference to the educational question. In the debate which ensued the Conservative-Nationalist alliance which had been so carefully forged in the 1911 election showed its first signs of strain. The official Liberal position was an attack on the financial terms. Sharpest criticism of the legislation, however, came from some of Borden's own supporters led by P. E. Lamarche, a Conservative of distinct Nationalist leanings. Lamarche expressed strong disapproval of the Government's failure to provide constitutional guarantees for Catholic schoools in Keewatin. At the same time his ridicule of the Liberals' record on the Manitoba school question made it clear that he was deserting his allies without joining the enemy.[87] F. D. Monk, speaking for the Government, replied to the French-Canadian critics by declaring that the federal authorities could not force Manitoba to provide guarantees for separate schools which had no legal existence prior to the transfer.[88] Yet a faint spark of hope for the minority was ignited by the Prime Minister and two of the French-Canadian ministers, Monk, and L. P. Pelletier. Each of these speakers emphasized the view that the

[83]*Ibid.*, James Whitney to Frank Cochrane, Jan. 12, 1912; *Manitoba Free Press*, Nov. 22, 1911.

[84]Canada, House of Commons, *Debates*, 1911–12, II, 3528.

[85]P.A.C., Borden Papers, OCA 43, Archbishop Langevin to Borden, Jan. 29, 1912.

[86]*Ibid.*, Borden to Archbishop Langevin, Feb. 3, 1912; Bishop Charlebois to Borden, Jan. 31, 1912, and reply, Feb. 14, 1912.

[87]Canada, House of Commons, *Debates*, 1911–12, II, 4406.

[88]*Ibid.*, 4417.

Manitoba Government could be depended upon to deal justly with the Catholic minority.[89]

This was a vague promise, but events were moving in Manitoba in a way which seemed to give it substance. It was during the spring of 1912 that the Manitoba legislature adopted certain changes in the School Act which came to be known as the Coldwell amendments. Though these modifications were not free from ambiguity, they appeared to offer some relief to the Roman Catholics by permitting the separation of Protestant and Catholic children in the larger schools.[90] The origin of these amendments has always been a "mystery,"[91] but a clue is found in a letter written by the Archbishop of St. Boniface to Col. Alphonse Audet, a Conservative party organizer in Montreal, who no doubt was in close touch with Borden's French-Canadian supporters. Mgr Langevin, on the advice of Audet, had proposed certain amendments to the School Act to Roblin and Rogers, and his suggestions had found acceptance. It had been agreed that the number of scholars required before a petition for a Catholic teacher could be presented should be reduced from forty to twenty-five. In addition the clause which prohibited the separation of pupils on religious lines was to be indirectly repealed. Mgr Langevin was jubilant, for this was only the beginning: "Roblin et ses partisans ont *accepté cette dernière rédaction des clauses*; mais il est bien entendu avec mes catholiques moi-même et Roblin que c'est un simple *commencement de restauration de nos droits scolaires.*"[92] Though disappointed by the performance of Monk and the French Conservatives in the Keewatin settlement, he was nevertheless very pleased that a gain had been made for his flock through these changes. The fact that this agreement was made and carried out at least partially vitiates the repeated claim made by Laurier and the Manitoba Liberals that the Roblin Government was insincere in its promises to the Manitoba Catholics.

More than merely providing a clue to the mystery of the Coldwell amendments Mgr Langevin's revelation seems to suggest the method by which the leaders of the Conservative party were able to maintain the support of the Quebec wing. Though the Keewatin legislation briefly disturbed party cohesion, the Coldwell amendments helped to set matters right. The key man in these events must have been Robert Rogers who could exert his influence at both

[89]*Ibid.*, 4420, 4444, 4492.

[90]Morton, "The Manitoba Schools and Canadian Nationalism," 55.

[91]Morton, *Manitoba*, 325.

[92]Archbishop Langevin to Colonel Alphonse Audet, 31 mars 1912 in L. Groulx, ed., "Correspondance Langevin-Audet," *Revue d'Histoire de l'Amérique Française,* I, (1947) 2, 277.

Ottawa and Winnipeg. Another incident which suggests that there was hard work being done to prevent any public breach in the Conservative ranks over the Manitoba school question was a banquet held in Winnipeg on April 12, 1912. Here again one suspects the hand of Rogers working to provide a public exhibition of Conservative party solidarity. The purpose of the celebration was to honour Premier Roblin for his successful settlement of the boundary extension question. In attendance were five notable French-Canadian politicians, led by the Nationalists, P. E. Lamarche, M.P., and Armande Lavergne. Dr. Eugene Paquet, M.P., J. H. Rainville, M.P. and Louis Coderre, M.P. filled out the complement.[93] The ghost of racial disharmony which had raised its ugly head in the Keewatin debate had been successfully excluded from the feast.

Thus the schism in the Borden coalition which had threatened as a result of the Manitoba school question had been averted. Premier Borden had successfully dealt with the first crisis of his administration and maintained racial harmony within his party, a task which was to become increasingly difficult for him. But while national unity had been preserved a price had to be paid, as is not an infrequent result when this principle is invoked in Canadian politics. As events transpired the long-suffering minority in Manitoba gained little from this compromise,[94] and their rights were soon further limited by a new educational enactment under the Norris Liberal administration.[95] In looking at the position of the minority at the end of these years it is difficult to avoid the conclusion that their interests ranked second to the exigencies of party politics. This was the despairing conclusion of the journal of the English-speaking Catholics in Manitoba: "The treatment that has been meted out to us in the last 22 years at the hands of this or that political party is guarantee enough that the future holds very little for us. When one party is willing to enact legislation to restore our Catholic schools, the other invariably refuses to fall in line and the efforts and good will of the first are thereby paralysed."[96]

In justice to the politicians involved in these events, it should be added that it was the illiberality of the majority of the people in Manitoba that made this political game possible. Faced with an electorate which refused to accept cultural duality, the politicians readily succumbed to the temptation to sacrifice minority rights on the altar of political success.

[93]Ross, *Roblin*, 132; Rumilly, *Histoire*, XVII, 95.
[94]*Canadian Annual Review*, 1913, 562–3.
[95]Morton, *Manitoba*, 351.
[96]*North West Review*, March 2, 1912.

The Campaign for a French Catholic School Inspector in the North-West Territories, 1898-1903

MANOLY R. LUPUL

MUCH HAS BEEN WRITTEN ABOUT the Manitoba school question since Sir Charles Tupper failed to carry the 1896 general election on a platform of remedial legislation for that province's aggrieved Roman Catholic minority.[1] Some attention has also been given to the less dramatic North-West school question which held the national stage briefly in 1894, after Sir John Thompson's Conservative government refused to disallow the School Ordinance (passed in December 1892) establishing state control of public education in the North-West Territories.[2] Little, however, has been written about subsequent developments, particularly those in the North-West. Of these, perhaps the most interesting are the negotiations between the Roman Catholic Church and the governments at Regina and Ottawa over the appointment of a French Catholic school inspector. During a five-year period church efforts, on occasion, approached the heroic. Neither government yielded, however, and the church came away empty-handed, only to regroup its forces for the next encounter.

The inspectoral issue had its roots in a school law passed by the territorial Legislative Assembly in January 1892, transferring the

[1] Even so, a definitive account of the Manitoba school question, including not only the crucial years 1890–96 but subsequent developments well into the twentieth century, has still to be written. For an outline of the principal developments, see C. B. Sissons, *Church and State in Canadian Education* (Toronto, 1959), chap. III.

[2] See M. R. Lupul, "Relations in Education Between the State and the Roman Catholic Church in the Canadian North-West with Special Reference to the Provisional District of Alberta from 1880 to 1905," unpublished Ph.D. thesis, Harvard University, 1963.

Reprinted from *Canadian Historical Review*, XLVIII (4), December, 1967

appointment and control of school inspectors from the Protestant and Roman Catholic sections of the Board of Education to the Lieutenant Governor in Council.[3] Of the four inspectors appointed in March, only one, the Reverend David Gillies, was a Catholic. Frederick W. G. Haultain, leader of the Assembly's Executive Committee (Executive Council after 1897) and *de facto* premier of the North-West Territories, considered the single appointment fair, for there were only 44 Catholic and 286 Protestant schools in the territories at the time.[4] The inspectors were paid annual salaries and were considered permanent officials of the government.[5] On a tour of inspection in northern Alberta in April 1892, the Reverend Gillies gave Bishop Vital Grandin of St. Albert to understand that he was an officer of the government, not a Catholic inspector.[6] Finding the dual role of parish priest and school inspector too exhausting,[7] Gillies resigned in April 1894 and was succeeded by James Calder,[8] a Moose Jaw teacher who later became Saskatchewan's first minister of education. The "real" motive for Gillies' resignation, Archbishop Adélard Langevin of St. Boniface declared later, was his "failing health" and his "impression that there was a pressure in certain quarters to bring him to follow the Normal School course at Regina."[9] But Charles H. Mackintosh, the governor, blamed the resignation on "the hierarchy objecting to his acting under the present ordinance." The move was "foolish" because Gillies was the "only" qualified candidate the minority could offer. Sir John Thompson agreed that "pressure from St. Boniface, in order to make a difficult situation more difficult," had brought about the resignation.[10]

Since 1894, then, Roman Catholic public and separate schools in the territories had been inspected by non-Catholic school inspectors. Early in 1898, when the Manitoba school question had reached a stalemate, Archbishop Langevin re-opened the North-West school question when he asked Haultain to appoint "a Catholic Inspector, subject to the approval of the Bishops concerned." Haultain replied in general terms, promising to present the archbishop's request to the

[3]*Ordinances of the North-West Territories*, 1891–92, No. 28, s. 5.
[4]Public Archives of Canada (P.A.C.), Sir John Thompson Papers, Haultain to Thompson, unofficial, Nov. 28, 1893.
[5]Saskatchewan Archives (S.A.), Minutes of the Executive Committee, March 21, July 13, 1892.
[6]Oblate Archives, Edmonton (O.A.), Bishop Grandin's Journal, April 30, 1892.
[7]Archbishop's Archives, St. Boniface (A.A.St.B.), Gillies to Archbishop Taché, Dec. 26, 1893.
[8]S.A., Minutes of the Executive Committee, April 13, 1894.
[9]A.A.St.B., Memorandum of Archbishop Langevin, "How was kept the promise of the Hon. M. Haultain for the appointment of a catholic inspector in the North-West Territories," Nov. 9, 1901. Cited hereafter as Langevin Memorandum.
[10]Thompson Papers, Mackintosh to Thompson, private and confidential, April 14, 1894, and vol. 43, 401, Thompson to Mackintosh, April 24, 1894.

next meeting of the Council of Public Instruction, the administrative body consisting of the four-man Executive Committee and four non-voting advisory members (two Protestants and two Roman Catholics) responsible for education.[11] Late in August, Bishop Grandin directed Father Albert Lacombe (then in eastern Canada) to contact officials at the University of Ottawa regarding a suitable candidate.[12] Archbishop Langevin followed with an appeal to Prime Minister Laurier. Unless a bilingual school inspector were appointed soon, he declared, the French language would disappear in a region explored by Laurier's forefathers and evangelized by French-Canadian missionaries.[13] Within two days Langevin informed Grandin that Charles Caron would be the minority's candidate for the inspectoral post: "Il n'est que tonsuré; mais il est aussi instruit que m. Gillies. Il ne lui donne pas le titre de *Révérend*! C'est Monsieur Caron tout court."[14] With the Assembly in session at Regina, letters to Governor Mackintosh, Haultain, Daniel Maloney (member for St. Albert), and Charles Boucher (member for Batoche) were hurriedly dispatched, each pressing Caron's candidacy.[15]

The government, Langevin told Haultain, had "always" given the minority to understand that a Catholic school inspector would be appointed as soon as the minority presented a competent candidate. Although he had been "too busy" to give the matter much attention after Gillies' resignation, he now had a candidate "well fitted" for the position. Caron came from Sherbrooke, Quebec, and knew "*English* better than French." He had completed the classical course, had taught for more than twenty years, and was "one time principal of a school in Montreal." Although "perfectly" qualified, he was "quite ready to undergo an examination if required. In case you should accept him as Inspector *pro tem.*, at least, I will send him a word to come at once." The tone of Langevin's letter makes it clear that he regarded the appointment a mere formality. His letter to Maloney was even more brusque: "There is no question of speaking in the House about it—try to get your personal friends, and all those who depend on Catholic voters, to join in that matter the Catholic members—Be kind and nice, but firm as a rock—*We must have it.*" If Gillies' resignation were raised, Boucher was instructed to say that Gillies knew only English and that the minority had a right to a bilingual inspector. Above all, there should be no delay on the pretext that Caron had not passed the normal school examinations in the terri-

[11]A.A.St.B., Langevin to Haultain, n.d., and Haultain's reply, March 22, 1898.
[12]O.A., 22 août 1898.
[13]P.A.C., Laurier Papers, 4 sept. 1898.
[14]Archbishop's Archives, Edmonton (A.A.E.), 6 sept. 1898.
[15]The letter to Mackintosh has not been seen, but it is mentioned in *ibid*. The other letters are in A.A.St.B., Letter Book, 1895–1900, 232, 226, and 224, Sept. 7, 1898.

tories; he would do so after he was appointed. There was nothing to fear; Caron was well educated.

Bishop Grandin and Father Hippolyte Leduc, Grandin's chief administrative assistant who had attacked the 1892 School Ordinance in a bitter pamphlet released in 1896,[16] had doubted Haultain would make the appointment,[17] and their doubts were soon confirmed by Maloney. Haultain and several members of the Assembly "fully" admitted the justice of the minority's request, but they would not be "dictated to . . . as they knew of others qualified for the position." The minority itself was to blame for not having a Catholic inspector. After the church had "forced" Gillies to resign, ". . . there was no qualified man belonging to our Church to fill the position."[18] Langevin advised Grandin to work for Maloney's defeat: ". . . on sent un pauvre diable sans influence qu'est sous la cause des Protestants."[19] Langevin soon heard from Haultain himself. He was glad to learn of Caron's candidacy, but Langevin was "under a slight misapprehension" regarding the government's position:

We have never undertaken to appoint a Catholic School Inspector, except in the case of a vacancy, and such a vacancy does not exist at present. If such a vacancy should occur, other things being equal, I should incline to the appointment of a man possessing such special qualifications as you attribute to Mr. Caron. In all probability, within a year, our school work will have so increased that another inspector will be needed; in such an event, or in the event of a vacancy occurring in the meantime, I shall be only too glad to consider Mr. Caron as an applicant for the position.[20]

Political developments unexpectedly intervened in the minority's favour. In September, after less than four months in office, Lieutenant Governor M. C. Cameron, Mackintosh's successor, died, and Amédée E. Forget, a Regina barrister who had sought the office earlier,[21] was again a contender. Since 1876 Forget had held several important government posts, demonstrating in each his devotion to French Catholic interests. Accordingly, Archbishop Langevin wired Laurier immediately that Forget's appointment would be agreeable to the episcopate and important for the school question.[22] To Forget, Langevin made it clear that "le premier fruit" of his nomination would be "un inspecteur français": "Je le demande au nom du patriotisme aussi bien qu'au nom de la religion."[23] The government acted quickly and

[16]H. Leduc, *Hostility Unmasked: School Ordinance of 1892 of the North-West Territories and Its Disastrous Results* (Montreal, 1896).

[17]O.A., Grandin à Langevin, 12 sept. 1898.

[18]A.A.St.B., Maloney to Langevin, Sept. 17, 1898.

[19]A.A.E., 26 sept. 1898.

[20]*Ibid.*, Sept. 24, 1898.

[21]Laurier Papers, Forget à Laurier, *privée*, 26 jan. 1898.

[22]*Ibid.*, telegram, 27 sept. 1898.

[23]A.A.St.B., Letter Book, 1895–1900, 288, *personnelle*, 28 sept. 1898.

Forget became governor on October 13. From Ottawa, Lacombe informed Grandin that Laurier was happy the appointment pleased the clergy.[24] Laurier also approved of Caron's candidacy, Lacombe said, but wished it known that he was not "seul maître" of the schools in the Canadian west. Local governments, except in certain exceptional cases, could not be controlled from Ottawa.[25]

With a friendly incumbent in Government House, Bishop Grandin sent his coadjutor, Emile J. Legal, to see Haultain at Regina. Haultain and James A. Ross, the other resident member of the Executive Council, gave Legal to understand that, provided a suitable candidate were available, the government "espéraient pouvoir appointer un inspecteur parlant français & anglais" — and this, Legal added, "dans l'espace de 6 mois."[26] There was no definite commitment, however; nor was there any indication that the bilingual inspector would be Catholic and/or French. Early in 1899, at Legal's request, Laurier wrote Forget and was advised that a private word to Haultain would be well received. Ross favoured the minority more than Haultain, but both were disposed to name "un Inspecteur d'écoles catholiques," as there was a vacancy.[27] Archbishop Langevin also wrote Laurier to remind him of his promise to have "un inspecteur catholique et français" appointed in the North-West. With Forget and Ross in Ottawa to negotiate the territorial budget, Laurier had "une excellente occasion de faire admettre le *principe* de la *nomination* par ceux qui dépendent de vous en tant de manières." At Forget's request, he had withdrawn Caron's candidacy and was seeking another candidate, who should be named if Laurier found him acceptable.[28]

En route to St. Boniface from an episcopal meeting in Calgary, Langevin dined at the governor's residence on March 11, with Haultain, Ross, G. H. V. Bulyea (a non-resident member of the Executive Council), and Dr. D. J. Goggin, the Chief Superintendent of Schools and Director of the Normal School at Regina. The government, he learned, was prepared to appoint "un inspecteur *catholique*, sachant le français," who should have "quelque chose d'équivalent à un certificat de première classe *professional*, et aussi, si possible, un degré universitaire."[29] The main problem was to find a suitable candidate.

Having dropped Caron's candidacy, Langevin asked Father H. A. Constantineau, Rector of the University of Ottawa, and Archbishop

[24]A.A.E., 20 oct. 1898.   [25]*Ibid.*, 3 nov. 1898.
[26]Oblate Archives, Ottawa, Legal à Langevin, 23 déc. 1898 (microfilm).
[27]Laurier Papers, Legal à Laurier, *personnelle*, 5 jan. 1899. Laurier's letter to Forget has not been seen. The account is based on Legal à Laurier, *privée*, 26 jan. 1899, in the Laurier Papers.
[28]*Ibid.*, 2 fév. 1899.
[29]A.A.E., Langevin à Grandin, 11 mars 1899.

Paul Bruchési of Montreal to find a replacement. Each presented his own candidate (Bruchési presented two) and, much to Langevin's surprise, both resented the division of responsibility. Bruchési, working on the assumption that the main consideration was a candidate satisfactory to the bishops, viewed the University's candidate as a challenge to episcopal authority. Langevin was dismayed: Bruchési, he wrote Grandin, did not realize that ". . . nous ne sommes pas les maîtres à Régina!"[30] The matter came to a head when Lacombe wrote Constantineau and requested a Bachelor of Arts degree for one of Bruchési's candidates. Embarrassed, the indignant rector replied that, even if the candidate knew both languages, held a normal school certificate, and was an experienced teacher (all of which he doubted), the arts degree could not be granted without submitting documents to the University Senate. The university would suffer if Protestant universities or the government could prove that Ottawa granted degrees without a rigorous display of competence. Moreover, with his own candidate's case well advanced, Constantineau criticized Bruchési for presenting still another candidate.[31] Aroused by Constantineau's audacity, Bruchési "a menacé de rompre" with Langevin.[32]

To complicate matters further, each of the three candidates—A. Bélanger (proposed by Constantineau), J. V. Desaulniers and G. Beaulieu (proposed by Bruchési)—lacked either adequate background, or professional training, or teaching experience. Bélanger held a B.A. degree from Ottawa, but had no normal school certificate. He had taught for three years in "the higher branches of a collegiate course . . . and . . . in the elementary departments of education."[33] The statement was vague and would not impress Haultain who had made it clear that the "main" part of the inspector's work was to inspect "ordinary public schools."[34] (In 1896 only 2 per cent of the territorial school population attended secondary school classes.[35]) Yet Bélanger was without 'ordinary' public school experience.[36] In place of a normal school certificate, he submitted "an official recommendation" from Dr. J. A. McCabe, principal of the Ottawa Normal School, which, he said, was "worth any Normal School certificate." At the

[30]*Ibid.*, 2 avril 1899.
[31]Lacombe's letter to Constantineau (25 mars 1899) has not been seen. The account is based on Constantineau's reply, A.A.St.B., 27 mars 1899.
[32]A.A.E., Langevin à Grandin, 2 avril 1899.
[33]Bélanger to Haultain, March 26, 1899, in Sessional Paper no. 8, unpublished sessional papers of the Council and the Legislative Assembly in the North-West Territories, microfilm no. 2.96, S.A. Cited hereinafter as Territorial Sessional Papers (T.S.P.).
[34]A.A.St.B., Haultain to Bélanger, March 21, 1899.
[35]*Report of the Council of Public Instruction of the North-West Territories 1896* (Regina, 1897), p. 13.
[36]A.A.St.B., Constantineau à Langevin, 18 mars 1899.

same time, he admitted he had already embarked on "a private course of applied psychology and pedagogy" from Dr. McCabe and his vice-principal: "This is the complement of my experience and will correct any deficiency under which I might labor." His written English lacked polish and did not strengthen the application.[37]

The first, and the more important, of the two candidates proposed by Bruchési also had his shortcomings. J. V. Desaulniers (the subject of Lacombe's letter to Constantineau) had studied in an unnamed college without university affiliation.[38] His professional qualifications were an "Academic Diploma, the highest award to teachers in the Province of Quebec, bearing the degree 'with distinction' for both French and English." He had taught for ten years, the last four as an assistant principal "in one of the highest Catholic Primary schools of Montreal—The Catholic Commercial Academy." Should the government "strongly urge upon the B.A.," he would do his best to pass "this examination before the Board of one of our Universities in a comparatively near future." However, he did not think he needed a degree because "the Examination papers for the Academic Diploma bear on the same subjects as for the B.A., together with Pedagogy." Desaulniers' written English was considerably better than Bélanger's.[39]

Even though G. Beaulieu, Bruchési's second candidate, presented himself as "utterly qualified for the position," he, too, had his deficiencies. He possessed a law degree from Laval University and was a member of the Quebec bar. He held a first-class teaching certificate from the Jacques Cartier Normal School in Montreal.[40] A teacher in the fifth form at the Montcalm School in Montreal, he lacked elementary school experience.[41] His reference to his teaching experience was brief: "I am teaching at present in one of the most important schools of Montreal." His written English was weak and pretentious: "I have been induced to apply for the situation by both religious and civil authorities of our Province, happy, however, I would be to devote my time and energy to the noble cause of education in the vast plains of the West."[42]

Each of the three candidates was prepared to do Archbishop Langevin's bidding. Bélanger saw himself as Langevin's protégé and assured him he would exert every effort to be worthy of the position and of the archbishop's confidence. Beaulieu was as loyal: "De nouveau je proteste de mon entière soumission à votre Grandeur et vous réitère

[37]T.S.P., Sessional Paper no. 8, Bélanger to Haultain, March 26, 1899.
[38]A.A.St.B., Desaulniers à Langevin, 5 avril 1899.
[39]T.S.P., Sessional Paper no. 8, Desaulniers to Haultain, April 8, 1899.
[40]Ibid., Beaulieu to Haultain, April 11, 1899.
[41]A.A.St.B., Beaulieu à Langevin, 6 avril 1899, and Letter Book, 1895–1900, 517, Langevin à Villeneuve, 14 avril 1899.
[42]T.S.P., Sessional Paper no. 8, Beaulieu to Haultain, April 11, 1899.

le désir que j'aurais de travailler, dans le Nord-Ouest, aux chers intérêts de la religion catholique et de la nationalité canadienne-française."
In praising his friend (Beaulieu), the more reserved Desaulniers also
showed he knew what was expected of one who received the appointment: "Il serait prêt à mettre sa plume et ses connaissances tant légales
que pedagogiques au service de la cause catholique et nationale."[43]

On April 1, 1899, the minority was startled to learn that Duncan
P. McColl, principal of the public high school at Regina, was appointed
to the inspectoral staff.[44] Forget wrote Langevin that Haultain had
found Bélanger's certificates "excellents mais insuffisants." The minority
might be more fortunate in July when the next appointment would
probably be made.[45] To Father Lacombe, the delay meant there was
still time to obtain a baccalaureate for Desaulniers, whom he favoured,
believing him to be, as he put it, "encore plus *smart* que Mr. Forget."[46]
Negotiations with Laval University began on April 14 and four
days later Desaulniers had his degree. Lacombe gave Langevin the
following explanation: "Le document est obtenu simplement, sur
notre demande, sans autre formalité. Mais c'est un secret entre nous.
Il faut que notre candidat soit reconnu comme ayant obtenu le B.A.
après avoir subi les examens voulus."[47] On April 24 Desaulniers informed Haultain he had obtained the B.A. degree, after passing his
examination "before the Board of the Laval University."[48] Langevin
followed with a recommendation to Haultain, placing considerable
emphasis on Desaulniers' newly acquired degree. He also urged
Frédéric Villeneuve (St. Albert), Charles Fisher (Batoche), and
Benjamin Prince (Battleford) to support Desaulniers' candidacy in
the Assembly now in session at Regina.[49]

Haultain, suspecting Lacombe's ruse, told Villeneuve that Desaulniers' degree had "tout l'air d'un service qu'on veut rendre aux évêques"
and declined to appoint him.[50] On May 13 Desaulniers, without
explanation, asked Haultain to return his documents.[51] Lacombe, who
had counselled Desaulniers to withdraw, was not too disturbed. Bruchési's second candidate, Beaulieu, whom he termed "un vrai gentilhomme et très bien *posté*," was still in the running.[52] Langevin, in
turn, consoled himself by terming Desaulniers "un gentilhomme et un

[43]A.A.St.B., 4, 10, 8 avril 1899.
[44]*North-West Territories Gazette*, April 15, 1899, p. 1.
[45]A.A.St.B., 11 avril 1899.
[46]*Ibid.*, Lacombe à Langevin, 14 avril 1899.
[47]*Ibid.*, 19 avril 1899.
[48]T.S.P., Sessional Paper no. 8, April 24, 1899.
[49]A.A.St.B., Langevin to Haultain, April 25, 1899; Letter Book, 1895–1900, 566,
Langevin à Grandin et Legal, 24 avril 1899.
[50]O.A., Grandin à Langevin, 11 mai 1899.
[51]T.S.P., Sessional Paper no. 8, May 13, 1899.
[52]A.A.St.B., Lacombe à Langevin, 18 mai 1899.

Chrétien bien vertueux" for telling Haultain he had no degree. Haultain has acted "fort *malhonnêtement*; ce n'est pas un homme *bien recommandable*."[53]

All hope now rested with Beaulieu and no efforts were spared to get him appointed. First Villeneuve, then Laurier was contacted.[54] Laurier told Constantineau he could do little, as Haultain was "not a particular friend" of his. He would, however, write Ross, upon the latter's return from the District of Athabaska, where he and Father Lacombe were negotiating an Indian treaty.[55] Villeneuve and Prince informed Haultain that, after examining Beaulieu's application, they believed him to be "well qualified" for the position.[56] On Senator Dandurand's suggestion,[57] Legal saw Ross several times in Edmonton early in September. Ross expressed surprise that no appointment had been made and promised to look into the matter. In his report to Langevin, Legal for the first time noted the main reason for the delay. Villeneuve had learned from Haultain and Forget that the opening of many new schools had drained the territorial treasury. The government did not have the funds to meet the salary of a French Catholic school inspector.[58]

Disturbed, Langevin wrote Haultain and insisted he had "promised" in February and in May that "a Catholic inspector knowing French" would be appointed in July. With Ross back, there was no need for further delay. Ross, in turn, was asked to "hasten the thing now." All obstacles mentioned by Haultain had been removed, "and anyhow, where there is a will there is a way." Langevin urged Forget to do his utmost: "Oserait-on se moquer de nous! Et cela en face d'un Gouverneur catholique et français!"[59] Forget and Haultain, in reply, attributed the delay to economic exigencies. Forget explained that the government's hopes for an increase in the federal subsidy had not been realized. The government, Haultain declared, instead of adding to its staff, was considering a "large" reduction.[60] Exasperated, Grandin criticized Forget sharply and revealed, for the first time, that Joseph Royal, the French Catholic governor of the territories from 1888 to 1892, had also left something to be desired: "Je crois que M. Forget comme M. Royal laissent faire les choses sans s'occuper beaucoup du

[53]*Ibid.*, Letter Book, 1895–1900, 599, Langevin à Lacombe, 22 mai 1899.

[54]O.A., Grandin à Villeneuve, 25 juin 1899; Laurier Papers, Constantineau à Laurier, 10 juil. 1899.

[55]*Ibid.*, Laurier to Constantineau, July 11, 1899.

[56]T.S.P., Sessional Papers no. 8, July 12, 1899.

[57]A.A.St.B., R. Dandurand à Langevin, 2 août 1899.

[58]*Ibid.*, 11 sept. 1899.

[59]*Ibid.*, Langevin to Haultain, to Ross, to Forget, all dated Sept. 18, 1899.

[60]*Ibid.*, Forget à Langevin, 21 sept. 1899; T.S.P., Sessional Paper no. 8, Haultain to Langevin, Sept. 28, 1899.

gouvernement. Je ne sais pour quoi ces personnages portent le titre de gouverneur."[61]

Although the government could hardly expect the frustrated church authorities to accept its explanations at face value, its financial position was serious. Despite the large influx of settlers since 1896 (the first fruit of Sir Clifford Sifton's energetic immigration policies), the federal grant in 1899 ($282,879) was just 53 per cent of the amount requested ($535,000), the lowest percentage since 1892–93. Moreover, the size of the grant had not changed since 1897.[62]

Clearly, then, it was the federal government that was frustrating the minority's plans. Accordingly, Archbishop Langevin appealed to Laurier's faith and patriotism to furnish from the public treasury the twelve hundred dollars needed for the inspector's salary.[63] When Laurier said nothing, Legal, in Ottawa late in November, saw Laurier and gave him a memorandum on the subject.[64] From Regina, early in the year (1900), Ross gave Laurier the territorial government's position on the question: "When a new appointment is made we will keep in view the suggestions made by the French Roman Catholics but must submit that at present when we are unable to keep up the necessary liberal school grants, it is a bad time for them to press us for an appointment."[65] The minority's pressure, however, did not abate. On January 12 Legal wrote Haultain again and blamed Regina, not Ottawa, for the delay: "We managed in such a way that the Government at Ottawa was willing to supply the necessary sum for the salary. But even now the appointment has not been made & I do not [know] what will be the next objection."[66] When Langevin advanced the same line, Haultain countered that the territorial government "had no indication of any move on the part of the Federal Government to increase our grant in any way, and the object of my proposed visit to Ottawa is to call the attention of the Government to the very serious financial condition we are in." He suggested a meeting in Winnipeg during a stopover on his way east.[67] A meeting was arranged for February 2,[68] but none apparently was held. Legal could not understand the government's continued financial embarrassment. He wrote Langevin that Laurier had told him personally last November

[61]O.A., Grandin à Langevin, 5 oct. 1899.
[62]C. C. Lingard, *Territorial Government in Canada; The Autonomy Question in the Old North-West Territories* (Toronto, 1946), Appendix, p. 258.
[63]Laurier Papers, 28 oct. 1899.
[64]*Ibid.*, 29 nov. 1899.
[65]*Ibid.*, personal, n.d. For evidence that the letter was written early in 1900, see A.A.St.B., Forget à Langevin, 31 déc. 1899.
[66]T.S.P., Sessional Paper no. 8, Jan. 12, 1900.
[67]*Ibid.*, Jan. 17 and 25, 1900.
[68]A.A.St.B., Haultain to Langevin, Jan. 30, 1900.

that he had written Regina offering the salary. Moreover, "on a songé à un autre [prétexte]": appointees to the inspectoral staff had to reside in the west; they could not be imported from eastern Canada.[69]

Alphonse LaRivière, Member of Parliament for Provencher in Manitoba (where Langevin's episcopal see was located), saw Haultain in Ottawa on February 16 and learned that he would make the appointment if the federal government increased the territorial sub- sidy. As the government could not earmark funds for the purpose, LaRivière suggested to Langevin that he ask Laurier to enter into a special arrangement with Haultain when the subsidy was increased.[70] It is quite possible the minority's aspirations were now at the mercy of political considerations. The inspector's salary was not, after all, a major financial item. It is reasonable to suppose that had Haultain really desired to make the appointment, some way could have been found to do so. A lifelong Conservative in federal politics,[71] Haultain, however, may have decided to embarrass the Liberals by forcing them to specify a sum for a Catholic inspector. With the scars of the last western school controversy still visible and another election on the horizon, Laurier would not wish to revive the school question by allocating funds to suit French Catholic interests. If Haultain had no intention of appointing a French Catholic inspector he was in a good position to delay indefinitely. He could always claim a shortage of funds, and any increase in the federal subsidy could always be dis- posed of on any one of the numerous projects which the growth of population required.

The longer the government delayed, the more impatient the clergy became. Legal sent Haultain a third letter on February 28, which was followed two weeks later by another from Langevin expressing satis- faction at the government's increased subsidy for 1900.[72] The increase, Haultain admitted in reply, was "considerable" (the government granted $424,879 out of the $600,000 requested[73]); he hoped it would enable the government "to perfect our establishment in our Educa- tional Department, as well as in other directions." To Legal, he explained that his correspondence with Langevin on "all" matters precluded an earlier reply. As soon as finances permitted, the govern- ment would be "perfectly willing . . . to take into consideration the desirability of appointing a man who, in addition to other necessary qualifications, should possess the very useful qualification of being

[69]*Ibid.*, 10 fév. 1900.
[70]*Ibid.*, 17 fév. 1900.
[71]Lingard, *Territorial Government in Canada*, 117n.
[72]T.S.P., Sessional Paper no. 8, Feb. 28 and March 15, 1900.
[73]Lingard, *Territorial Government in Canada*, Appendix, p. 258.

able to speak French and other things being equal, would be pleased to be able to appoint a Roman Catholic, in deference to the sentiment of a large and important class of school rate-payers in the Territories."[74] Exasperated, Langevin wrote Grandin of the premier's letter: "C'est fabuleux." Having promised formally to appoint an inspector, Haultain now spoke vaguely of perfecting departmental personnel: "Est-ce de la sottise! Est-ce préméditation!"[75] To Haultain himself, he termed the letter "rather mysterious and almost discouraging."

> You know the qualified candidate we have proposed; you have received a considerable increase to your subsidy; what reasons can you bring to refuse us what we ask for so earnestly and so justly?
> It becomes burdensome for me, and perhaps for you also, to be always pressing, urging the matter. I expect to deal with a gentleman whose word of honor is sacred, consequently, as there is no more obstacle on the way, if nothing is done now, I will be justified with my venerable colleagues in considering it a denial of justice, and we will have to act consequently.[76]

Legal, although equally peeved, issued no threats. He knew "positively," he told Haultain, that ". . . the salary of a new inspector has been offered by the authorities at Ottawa, and if the federal aid to the Government of the Territories has been increased, it is partly with that end in view."[77] Haultain ignored Legal, but, in a strong letter, gave Langevin to understand that the government would not tolerate church interference in the conduct of territorial affairs: "We do not contemplate any immediate addition to our staff of Inspectors and although you have pointed out that we have obtained some financial assistance from Ottawa the question of our inability to indulge in further expenditure in any direction is one upon which we must exercise our own judgment."[78]

Relations between church and state were near the breaking point. The next step, Langevin confided to Grandin, was "une lutte sur les journaux," but for that he had "ni la capacité ni le courage."[79] In the Assembly, Charles Fisher requested in April that the government state its intentions on the question. Haultain quoted from his previous correspondence with Bishop Legal (March 23),[80] and, as no one pursued the matter, the minority's campaign was momentarily checked. In June Langevin asked Grandin to press Beaulieu's candidacy with Forget and the minority's friends in the Assembly, as it

[74]T.S.P., Sessional Paper no. 8, Haultain to Langevin, March 23, 1900, and Haultain to Legal, March 23, 1900.
[75]A.A.E., 26 mars 1900.
[76]A.A.St.B., Letter Book, 1895–1900, 912, March 27, 1900.
[77]April 5, 1900, copy enclosed in *ibid.*, Legal à Langevin, 5 avril 1900.
[78]*Ibid.*, April 10, 1900.   [79]A.A.E., 14 avril 1900.
[80]*Regina Standard*, April 11, 1900.

appeared a July appointment was imminent. But no letters were sent, and on June 30 A. M. Fenwick of Moose Jaw became the second Protestant teacher within a year to join the inspectoral staff.[81] Legal was amazed: "Voilà comment il [Haultain] utilise l'augmentation de l'allocation fédérale. On ne peut y mettre plus de désinvolture."[82] Langevin wrote Forget and threatened to place the whole matter before the public.[83] In a sarcastic letter to Haultain, Langevin expressed shock and disappointment at the recent appointment and wondered why news of the vacancy had been withheld. The minority's candidate could not have been the reason, for the government, or "at least" Haultain, had "previously admitted" that Beaulieu had "all" the necessary qualifications:

As for the question of money, you have, as you rightly said, to exercise your own judgment upon indulging in further expenditure; but I hope you will not find fault with me. Hon. and Dear Sir, if I recalled to your souvenir [sic] the very kind offer of the Head of the Federal Government in that respect. But, perhaps there was no question of an additional inspector, though in this case it seems to me that we have a certain right even to have a representative among the ordinary staff of inspectors, on account of the disadvantage under which our schools labour when no french speaking inspector visits them.

Perhaps also you did not find *other things equal*, and then you left aside a poor Roman Catholic candidate! There may be also other reasons that I do not know, and I would appreciate very much any information that you would judge proper to send me as an act of kindness on your part.

The minority had experienced "no strict injustice." Still, there was "every appearance of a lack of that real good will and that spirit of fair play," which he had "always" supposed Haultain to possess.[84]

Haultain, in reply, did not equivocate: ". . . none of the gentlemen who applied for the position of Inspector . . . possessed the qualifications which are considered necessary. . . ." Another vacancy existed, however, and if the "Church authorities" were "really anxious" to have "a Roman Catholic and French speaking Inspector," they might use their "undoubted" influence toward "inducing" qualified teachers to come west and "earn their promotion in the same way as other people are obliged to do." The minority had a number of "large and important" schools in the territories, "all of them sufficiently well to do to be able to afford to engage really first class teachers." Increased subsidies were "simply" the result of general territorial growth and had not been specified either "directly or indirectly" for the object Langevin suggested. He wished to assure the archbishop that he had "never" been actuated by "even an appearance of a lack of goodwill

[81]A.A.E., 18 juin 1900; *North-West Territories Gazette*, July 14, 1900, p. 1.
[82]A.A.St.B., Legal à Langevin, 19 nov. 1900.
[83]*Ibid.*, Letter Book, 1900, 478, 23 nov. 1900.
[84]*Ibid.*, Dec. 18, 1900.

and of fair play" toward the minority. On the other hand, a candidate could hardly expect an appointment "simply" because he was a Roman Catholic and spoke French.[85] Laurier, too, made it clear that Haultain and Ross were "tout à fait" disposed to make an appointment, if the candidate were "parfaitement compétent." Differences regarding competence would disappear if the Regina authorities were offered a candidate familiar with schooling in all parts of Canada.[86]

Haultain had finally made it clear that the lever of federal power would be no more effective in the territories than it had been in Manitoba in support of the minority's educational interests. "Il faut," Langevin wrote Legal, "*passer par* Régina: par les mains de *Goggin* pour être acceptable. C'est révoltant."[87] (Later in the year, in a memorandum on the question, Langevin remarked pointedly: "If it is required that the candidate to the inspectorship be *residing in the Territories* and acquainted with the *Normal training* given in Regina, why was not this condition specified at the very beginning!!"[88]) For most of the year (1901), the minority made little progress toward its goal. Two candidates—Lucien Dubuc, a young Edmonton lawyer with a B.A. degree but no teaching experience, and a Mr. Vendôme from Quebec, "un savant et un bon catholique"—were considered and rejected, the former for his political ambitions and the latter because of his weak English.[89] In April, after an unsuccessful trip to eastern Canada, Langevin revived Bélanger's candidacy and asked Legal to find him a teaching position in Alberta to meet the government's residence requirements.[90] The separate school trustees in Edmonton agreed to co-operate and Langevin approached Bélanger, noting that he could not avoid the normal school "du fameux Goggin, sorte de faux-ministre de l'instruction publique, âme damnée de Haultain, premier ministre."[91] Bélanger, however, was no longer interested. He was unwilling to exchange the security of a recent appointment at the University of Ottawa for the uncertainties of the territorial position.[92]

No further steps were taken until November 9, when Langevin, in a last major effort, drew up a memorandum intended for the directors of selected Catholic teacher training institutions in eastern Canada. In it he reviewed the minority's unsuccessful negotiations at Regina

[85]*Ibid.*, Jan. 18, 1901.
[86]*Ibid.*, Laurier à Langevin, 12 jan. 1901.
[87]*Ibid.*, Letter Book, 1900–1, 173, 24 jan. 1901.
[88]*Ibid.*, Langevin Memorandum.
[89]*Ibid.*, Letter Book, 1900–1, 173, Langevin à Legal, 24 jan. 1901; Legal à Langevin, 30 jan. 1901.
[90]*Ibid.*, Letter Book, 1900–1, 321, 3 avril 1901.
[91]*Ibid.*, Legal à Langevin, 12 avril 1901; Letter Book, 1900–1, 389, Langevin à Bélanger, 16 avril 1901.
[92]*Ibid.*, Bélanger à Langevin, 23 avril 1901.

since 1898, listed the inspector's qualifications, and appealed for "a good Catholic well recommended by his Bishop & his parish priest . . . a gentleman really competent and that [sic] will be entirely devoted to the prosperity of the Church!"[93] To circumvent the difficult residence requirements, he told Laurier that a satisfactory candidate should be placed on salary immediately, on the understanding he would assume no responsibilities until he had acquainted himself with the territorial school system.[94] On December 18, three days after Langevin and Legal had interviewed him, Langevin informed Laurier that L. E. O. Payment of Ottawa, a law student at Laval, would be the minority's next candidate. If Laurier found him satisfactory, Haultain could not refuse to name him, as ". . . rien ne lui manque, ce nous semble."[95] On December 23 Laurier agreed to forward Payment's application to Regina. Payment also secured the aid of Principal McCabe and two Members of Parliament, Frederick D. Monk, leader of the Conservative party in Quebec, and Rodolphe Lemieux, Laurier's future solicitor general (1904). The minority's strategy was the same as ever. Laurier was to impose the nomination on Haultain "comme condition de l'octroi d'une partie des subsides." To avoid counterplans, the minority would delay the application until the federal session had begun.[96]

Payment sent a copy of the application (a well-written, imposing document) to the archbishop for approval. He held a B.A. degree with the "highest honours" from the University of Ottawa. He had attended Prescott Model School in Ontario in 1887 and, on graduation, had received a strong recommendation from the principal. He had taught for more than a year in Ontario, and his work, according to a trustee's testimonial, had met with "the satisfaction of all concerned." The trustee described him as "a faithful, energetic, capable and inspiring teacher." From Ontario, Payment went to Manitoba, where, after teaching several months on an interim certificate, he attended a session at the normal school in Winnipeg, then (1890) under the "distinguished principalship" of D. J. Goggin. A letter from Goggin to Payment's father was enclosed; Payment had been judged " 'Excellent in every respect.' " Payment's professional training totalled six months. In Manitoba he had taught a year in "the Protestant Separate Schools," followed by three years in the public schools. During five and a half years at the University of Ottawa, he had held "a professorship of Mathematics, to which later was added that of Professor of

[93]*Ibid.*, Langevin Memorandum.
[94]Laurier Papers, 8 déc. 1901.
[95]A.A.E., Legal à Grandin, 15 déc. 1901; Laurier Papers, Langevin à Laurier, 18 déc. 1901.
[96]A.A.St.B., Payment à Langevin, 23 déc. 1901.

History, Geography, and Drawing." He had "ten and one half years" of teaching experience. He possessed "equal facility" in French and English and was the "Murray gold medallist" in English at the University in 1899. References from a trustee in Manitoba and the rectors of Ottawa (Father Constantineau) and Laval (the Reverend O. E. Mathieu) accompanied the application. He was applying, he said, at the "earnest sollicitations [sic]" of Langevin, Legal and Bishop Albert Pascal, the Vicar Apostolic of Saskatchewan.[97]

The modest application, calculated to impress, left out some pertinent details, however. Payment, a crusader on behalf of Catholic educational interests, had discussed the school question in Manitoba's newspapers in 1892 and was anxious to resume the role of a literary and legal knight errant in the Canadian west. If he were appointed, he told Langevin, he would establish Catholic normal schools, hire qualified and devoted teachers, and organize an educational journal to defend Catholic rights. He had already discussed his programme with the Reverend N. Dubois, principal of the Jacques Cartier Normal School in Montreal. Payment thought Langevin should contact Napoléon A. Belcourt, Member of Parliament for Ottawa, who had "des sympathies toutes spéciales" for Payment and much influence with Laurier.[98] Laurier was less sympathetic to Payment because the latter's brother, a former mayor of Ottawa, was disliked by the prime minister "au suprême degré."[99]

Langevin, pleased with the application, asked Payment to consult Monk and Lemieux about the admission that it was solicited by the clergy. The reference to legal studies might also be omitted: "Ils [Haultain and Goggin] auraient peur de se donner un maître."[100] Mindful of the Desaulniers incident, Langevin warned Grandin that Legal, not Lacombe, should advise the new candidate. Grandin should also ask Archbishop Diomède Falconio, the Apostolic Delegate in Ottawa, to use his influence with Laurier.[101] Grandin, by now deeply pessimistic,[102] wrote the delegate,[103] only to learn that Laurier found Payment's qualifications inadequate. Payment was pursuing legal, not pedagogical, studies, and he intended to join the bar as soon as possible. The minority had to propose a better qualified Catholic for the position.[104] Langevin now asked Laurier to persuade Haultain to

[97]Ibid., Payment to Haultain, n.d., 1902.

[98]Langevin did as advised: ibid., Letter Book, 1901-2, 157, Langevin à Belcourt, 14 jan. 1902; Belcourt à Langevin, 18 jan. 1902.

[99]Ibid., Payment à Langevin, 8 jan. 1902.

[100]Ibid., Letter Book, 1901-2, 140, 9 jan. 1902.

[101]Ibid., Letter Book, 1899-1902, 678, 9 Jan. 1902.

[102]O.A., Grandin à Langevin, 29 déc. 1901.

[103]Ibid., Grandin à Falconio, 15 jan. 1902.

[104]A.A.E., Falconio à Grandin, 29 jan. 1902.

make the appointment. It was "impossible" to find a better candidate than Payment.[105] Legal, in turn, appealed to both the delegate and Laurier. Although the School Ordinance sanctioned the principle of public and separate schools ("un double système"), the regulations of the Council of Public Instruction undermined the principle by allowing Protestants to inspect Catholic schools. Similarly, even though the law permitted the teaching of French, the parsimonious nature of the regulations and the illiteracy of the inspectors in French limited the benefits of the provision. It was "parfaitement en droit" to say that the first qualification of a school inspector should be knowledge of French as well as English. Payment's legal studies only rendered him more competent for the position. The ill will of the territorial government was so evident that Laurier had "parfaitement le droit" to impose the candidate, on Regina, especially as Payment had the confidence of the western hierarchy.[106]

Payment's case, however, was beyond the reach of protests and appeals. When Langevin advised Lemieux that "Sir Wilfrid a besoin d'être fortifié: il est trop délicat vis à vis du Premier du Nord-Ouest," Lemieux replied that Laurier disapproved of Payment, but would be pleased to recommend "tout autre candidat qu'il jugera plus acceptable."[107] Villeneuve's ill-timed personal appeal to Laurier (sent at Langevin's request), suggesting that Laurier use the lever of provincial autonomy (then gaining momentum in the territories) to persuade Haultain and A. L. Sifton, the territorial treasurer, to reconsider their negative attitude toward Payment's appointment, brought the curt reply that Haultain and Sifton were no longer in Ottawa and that, in any case, the minority would experience no difficulty if it presented an acceptable candidate.[108]

Legal blamed Laurier for the failure to obtain the appointment. Although a highly placed French Catholic, he was of little or no use to the church: "Que ces bons protestants et fanatiques du Nord-Ouest et du Manitoba et d'Ontario font bien de profiter de la présence d'un M. Laurier qui est toujours prêt à sanctionner ce qu'ils désirent et complotent contre les catholiques! Et quelle humiliation de se faire ainsi souffleter par l'un des nôtres!"[109] Langevin, too, condemned Laurier: "Voilà comment les intérêts catholiques et français sont soignés par un catholique et un Canadien-Français."[110] Payment agreed

[105]Laurier Papers, 12 fév. 1902.
[106]Ibid., Legal à Falconio, 15 fév. 1902; Legal à Laurier, 16 fév. 1902.
[107]A.A.St.B., Letter Book, 1901–2, 302, 20 fév. 1902 et réponse 27 fév. 1902.
[108]Ibid., Letter Book, 1901–2, 65, Langevin à Villeneuve, 24 déc. 1901; Laurier Papers, Villeneuve à Laurier, personnelle, 3 mars 1902, et réponse, 6 mars 1902.
[109]A.A.St.B., Legal à Langevin, 8 mars 1902.
[110]Ibid., Letter Book, 1901–2, 439, Langevin à Payment, 18 mars 1902.

—"L'ennemi, c'est lui"—and went on to give Langevin three reasons for Laurier's opposition to his appointment. First, Payment had told Laurier he was only concerned to have the principle of Catholic education and separate schools recognized in the West and would therefore hold the position only until another candidate could qualify. He had also criticized Manitoba's textbooks, and Laurier was afraid of the political repercussions following the religious dissensions which his appointment would create, especially as Payment was intent on claiming Catholic rights. Finally, he had openly opposed Laurier's politics in Quebec City.[111]

Although thwarted again, Archbishop Langevin would not concede defeat. He wrote Principal Dubois and asked that L. L. Legault, a teacher at the Montcalm School in Montreal who had earlier shown an interest in the position, submit his application.[112] With Legault still interested, Langevin advised him on procedure and in the process revealed how little he appreciated political realities. The Regina authorities, he said, would accept no one who had not passed through their Normal School, and they would not yield unless Laurier, who could force their hand "en les prenant pas la famine," agreed to impose a man of his own choice.[113] Next, as in 1899, Langevin resorted to personal contact. En route to St. Boniface after an episcopal meeting at St. Albert, he dined with Forget, Haultain, and Sifton at Government House on April 14 and learned that Haultain was not even aware of Payment's application. "A-t-il oublié? M. Laurier a-t il oublié aussi ou omis?" he asked Monk.[114] To render himself "aimable," Haultain had spoken of his French Huguenot origins on his father's side and his French Catholic origins on his maternal grandmother's side. Langevin found Sifton "dur, mordant et aigre; il m'a fait l'impression d'un Ontarien mal lêché et peu civilisé." The minority, Langevin concluded, would have to obtain an inspector from the ranks of its own French-speaking teachers. The minority also needed to increase its representation in the Assembly. Catholic leaders, he told Legal, had to summarize their objections, study their voters, and alert the faithful to support only candidates who favoured Catholic demands.[115]

Though Payment was still willing to come west and Langevin was willing to try to negotiate a double exchange (Payment's credentials for a Manitoba teaching certificate, followed hopefully by a territorial certificate), Payment would only come if the position were definitely

[111]*Ibid., personnelle,* 21 mars 1902.
[112]*Ibid.,* Letter Book, 1901–2, 437, 18 mars 1902.
[113]*Ibid.,* Dubois à Langevin, 26 mars 1902; Letter Book, 1901–2, 520, Langevin à Legault, 31 mars 1902.
[114]*Ibid.,* Letter Book, 1901–2, 539, 18 avril 1902.
[115]*Ibid.,* Letter Book, 1899–1902, 795, 15 avril 1902.

offered.[116] Meanwhile Legault and Lemieux saw Laurier, who forwarded Legault's papers to Haultain with a supporting letter,[117] where the matter ended. On June 18, on Father Lacombe's advice, a new candidate, M. J. O'Connor of Ottawa, submitted his credentials to Langevin. A University of Toronto graduate in arts and law with "First Class Honors," O'Connor claimed to hold "every grade of teacher's and Inspector's certificate that is issued in Ontario." He had twelve years' teaching experience in public and separate "Schools and Colleges" and had held the positions of principal and professor of French (and English) at various institutions. He enclosed an impressive number of references, including testimonials from Archbishop Duhamel of Ottawa and Father Lacombe, but admitted to having "mislaid" two of his "best" from the Archbishops of Toronto and Kingston. He was concerned that Haultain "take care" of his documents, as they were his " 'stock in trade.' " A lawyer with his "heart" in "Catholic Education," O'Connor was thirty-eight, married, and had six children. The application was not modest and it was apparent the candidate had moved about considerably.[118] In forwarding O'Connor's application to Haultain, Langevin admitted he did not know the candidate "personally," although he was "well recommended." Having been "so unsuccessful until now," he did not "dare to insist." With Haultain in England, Bulyea gave the standard reply: there was no immediate vacancy and an additional appointment would necessarily depend upon the available funds. O'Connor, meanwhile, should enter the teaching profession in the territories.[119]

Although four candidates—Payment, Legault, O'Connor, and one Letourneau (a student at the Jesuit College in St. Boniface[120])—were anxious to become inspectors, Langevin, at mid-year 1902, was powerless to press their candidacies because none had taught in the territories. As a result, the issue lay dormant until late in 1903, when L. L. Kramer, a Regina teacher, volunteered his services after learning that Langevin had referred to him earlier as a prospective candidate. Kramer did not have a university degree, but thought Ottawa might be "induced" to grant him one. He was, he told Langevin, on a "friendly footing" with educational officials in Regina, and, if appointed, would do "everything" in his power "to watch over and further the interests of our Catholic Schools."[121] Langevin was definitely

[116]*Ibid.*, Payment à Langevin, 25 avril 1902; Letter Book, 1901–2, 619, Langevin à Payment, 29 avril 1902; File "Ecoles 1903–1915," Payment à Langevin, n.d.
[117]*Ibid.*, Dubois à Langevin, 4 mai, 1902.
[118]*Ibid.*, O'Connor to Langevin, June 18, 1902.
[119]*Ibid.*, Letter Book, 1901–2, 857, June 22, 1902; Bulyea to Langevin, July 3, 1902.
[120]*Ibid.*, Letter Book, 1899–1902, 866, Langevin à Legal, 25 mai 1902.
[121]*Ibid.*, Nov. 23, 1903.

interested,[122] and Kramer submitted his application. His qualifications included a first-class non-professional teaching certificate, normal schooling under Principal McCabe, and seventeen years' teaching experience in Ontario and the North-West. Testimonials from an inspector, a trustee, a headmaster, and a "pastor," all from Ontario, were submitted.[123] When Langevin asked whether he could examine the children of French-speaking Catholics in French, Kramer admitted he could not, but intended "to take up the study of that beautiful language after New Years [sic]."[124] The admission was apparently sufficient, for Langevin terminated negotiations immediately. Even if Kramer had met the linguistic and academic criteria, however, it is doubtful whether an appointment would have been made. Because of the heterogeneous population and the diverse academic and professional backgrounds of the teachers, James Calder, Deputy Commissioner of Education since 1901, concluded in 1903 that, if the schools were to secure and maintain any degree of uniformity and unity of purpose in the territories, they would do so "only . . . through our inspectors."[125] A French-speaking Catholic school inspector who placed the interests of the bilingual Catholic clergy above the unilingual interests of the territorial government would hardly have been acceptable at Regina.

Kramer was the minority's last candidate during the territorial period. Failure to obtain the appointment of a French Catholic school inspector was, of course, a bitter disappointment to the Catholic leaders. The fact that the territorial government rather arbitrarily added to the qualifications which candidates had to present did not help their cause. It is difficult to say whether the government seriously intended to make an appointment. There is some evidence that the government was slightly piqued by the earlier resignation of the Reverend Gillies. It is also possible that the Conservative Haultain may have realized the predicament of the Ottawa Liberals and wished to embarrass them. Certainly the cost of a French Catholic school inspector would not have sent the government in Regina into bankruptcy! It is also possible that Haultain saw the minority's campaign as a useful lever to obtain additional financial concessions from the federal government. It is reasonably clear that, if the territorial government did intend to make the appointment, it became less enthusiastic as immigration from continental Europe increased. In view of the

122Ibid., Letter Book, 1903–4, 529, Langevin to Kramer, Nov. 28, 1903.
123Ibid., Kramer to Langevin, Dec. 3, 1903.
124Ibid., Letter Book, 1903–4, 607, Dec. 9, 1903, and Dec. 11, 1903.
125Report of the Department of Education of the North-West Territories 1903 (Regina, 1904) p. 21.

many nationalities settling in the North-West, the government was apprehensive about setting precedents.

The minority, too, must bear some of the responsibility for the government's failure to make the appointment. Catholic claims to the contrary, the candidates presented by the church lacked either adequate academic background, professional training, or teaching experience. Once the residency qualification was introduced, the minority's cause was doomed. The larger Catholic schools were staffed by teaching sisters and the one-room elementary schools offered little incentive for ambitious French-Canadian male teachers in Quebec. The Catholics had only two high schools in the territories (at Calgary and Edmonton), and there is some evidence that very few Catholic pupils attempted high school studies[126] preparatory to teaching in the elementary grades. The local source of French Catholic teachers therefore was quite inadequate—a fact which ultimately spelled defeat for the minority's bid to obtain a French Catholic school inspector in the Canadian North-West.

[126]The Lacombe separate school in Calgary and the St. Joachim separate school in Edmonton enrolled no high school pupils in 1896 (*Report of the Council of Public Instruction 1896*, Appendix D, p. 79). Lacombe enrolled its first high school pupil in 1898, St. Joachim in 1901. In 1903 Lacombe enrolled thirteen Catholic pupils in Standard VI (Grade X) and three in Standard VII (Grade XI) and St. Joachim seven in Standard VI. J. F. Weber, o.s.b., "Report on Separate Schools," n.p., n.d., mimeo., p. 11, in St. Thomas More College Library, Saskatoon, Saskatchewan.

The Ontario Bilingual Schools Issue:
Sources of Conflict

MARILYN BARBER

IN OCTOBER, 1910, the bilingual schools of Ontario became the centre of bitter public criticism and debate. Newspapers previously indifferent to the existence of such schools showed a sudden interest in their operation and the Ontario government quickly appointed a commissioner to investigate and report on conditions in the bilingual schools. The serious controversy which followed was not entirely unexpected. Although attracting little public notice, the interaction of conflicting interests had been building up pressure for several years. The explosive situation thus created illustrates how prejudice and extremism can foment strife if fundamental principles clash and prevent co-operation.

The use of French in the publicly supported schools of Ontario was potentially a very divisive issue. French Canadians living in Ontario believed that it was essential for their children to use and study French at school in order to gain a thorough knowledge and appreciation of the language. French-Canadian parents repeatedly declared that they wanted their children to learn English because they realized that a knowledge of English was necessary for life in an English-speaking province. But an important rider was always attached to these declarations; they did not want English to be taught at the expense of French. French was the mother tongue, the symbol of French-Canadian identity and pride, and it took precedence over English, the language of business and the dominant language of the country. On the other hand, not all English-speaking residents of Ontario were willing to accept the presence of French in Ontario schools. Many saw Canada as primarily and properly a Britannic nation and feared that French in the schools of Ontario would undermine the Anglo-Saxon character of the province.

For some time after Confederation, French was accepted in Ontario

Reprinted from *Canadian Historical Review*, XLVII (3), September, 1966

schools as completely convertible with English. In 1885, a regulation of the Ontario Department of Education for the first time made the study of English compulsory in all public schools and instructions were sent to inspectors and teachers giving detailed directions for a programme in English.[1] The new policy can be considered as part of a general movement towards increased central control and higher standards of education but the Liberal administration of Sir Oliver Mowat was undoubtedly also keeping a wary eye on the political barometer. The emotions and prejudices inflamed by the Riel controversy and the Jesuit Estates Act strengthened English-Canadian extremists in their determination to defend British and Protestant institutions. Dalton McCarthy took up a crusade to secure the abolition of the French language in Manitoba and the Northwest Territories, and Ontario Conservatives demanded "English only" in the schools of the province. As a result of the agitation the Mowat government appointed a commission to investigate the teaching of English, and, after receiving the Commission's report, the Department of Education issued special regulations governing language in Ontario schools. Under these 1890 regulations definite provision was made for French as a subject of study in school sections where the French language prevailed, and French might be used as the language of instruction and communication in Ontario schools if the pupils were unable to understand English.[2] However, in 1885 the study of English had been made compulsory. Now, in addition, the 1890 regulations required that English be the language of instruction except where impracticable. The use of French as the language of instruction and communication was meant to be only a temporary expedient, and it was intended that English should become the language of the school as soon as possible.[3] Until 1912 the Ontario bilingual or English-French schools, as they were more officially called, were schools in which French as well as English might be used according to the terms of these regulations.[4] The 1890 regulations

[1]Province of Ontario, *Report of the Royal Commission on Education in Ontario, 1950* (hereafter *Hope Commission Report*) (Toronto, 1950), pp. 398–9. See also Franklin A. Walker, *Catholic Education and Politics in Ontario* (Toronto, 1964), *passim*.
[2]*Hope Commission Report*, p. 401.   [3]*Ibid.*, p. 402.
[4]In the regulations no direct reference was made to the teaching of English in separate schools while the public school course of study was specifically mentioned. Although regulations of the Education Department applied equally to separate schools and to public schools, the wording of these regulations could easily give rise to a belief that separate schools were exempted. No direct mention was made of the separate schools because in 1890 when the regulations were formed there were very few separate schools in which French was used. By contrast, in 1912 there were 223 separate schools as compared to 122 public schools in which French was used. Since both French Canadians and English Canadians have frequently equated bilingual schools with separate schools, it must be emphasized that bilingual schools were not necessarily separate schools and separate schools were by no means all bilingual.

temporarily quelled the demand for "English only" in Ontario schools, but the language problem was not solved.

The tension created by friction between the two major ethnic groups of Canada continued to mount in the late nineteenth and early twentieth centuries. The question of separate schools in Manitoba, Alberta, and Saskatchewan produced successive bouts of bitter racial and religious animosity. The Boer War raised the issue of imperialism and loyalty to Britain in an even more contentious form. As clash followed clash, the moderate forces lost some of their confidence and their patience, and extremists became more prominent. In 1903 the Ligue Nationaliste was organized in Montreal by a small group of young intellectuals, including Armand Lavergne, Olivar Asselin, and Omer Héroux. Henri Bourassa, the unchallenged leader of this group, soon became the most prominent and commanding spokesman of the Nationalist movement. The Nationalists advocated an Anglo-French nation extending throughout Canada with provision for Catholic education and a general bilingualism in all provinces. In their efforts to further these aims the Nationalists maintained a clear-cut inflexible policy and made no allowance for those whose views differed from their own. It was an ambitious and active movement which, although small at first, appealed to French-Canadian youth. On the other hand, the unquestionably aggressive quality of the Nationalist programme strengthened the determination of many English-speaking Canadians to resist French encroachments.[5]

At this time of heightened sensitivity, both English-speaking and French-speaking residents of Ontario became acutely conscious of the new strength of Ontario's French-Canadian population. The influx of French Canadians into the eastern counties, which had aroused apprehension in the 1880's, had never ceased. As the French moved in, many English-speaking farmers, left in a minority and attracted by new opportunities in the West, moved out; their vacated farms were bought by French Canadians, and so, over the years, a gradual displacement process had converted much of Ontario's eastern corner into a French-speaking district.[6] Then, as lumbering activities and mineral discoveries opened up New Ontario, a considerable French-Canadian population moved across the Ottawa River and followed the railway lines along Ontario's northern fringe.[7] In addition, an isolated French-speaking group still dwelt in that section of Ontario first settled by the French—the southwestern counties of Essex and Kent.

[5]M. P. O'Connell, "The Ideas of Henri Bourassa," *Canadian Journal of Economics and Political Science*, XIX (1953), 361–76.

[6]O. D. Skelton, "The Language Issue in Canada," *Queen's Quarterly*, XXIV, 448. C. B. Sissons, *Bi-lingual Schools in Canada* (Toronto, 1917), pp. 85–6.

[7]Sissons, *Bi-lingual Schools*, p. 83.

The official census figures reveal that the French-speaking population of Ontario was not only growing but growing more rapidly than
the English-speaking population. While the total population of Ontario
rose from 1,926,922 to 2,523,274 between 1881 and 1911, the number
speaking French increased from 102,743 in 1881 to 158,671 in 1901 and
reached 202,442 in 1911. Moreover, it is likely that the French-speaking
population in 1911 exceeded the official census figure. In 1909 the
ecclesiastical census of the province reported 247,000 French Canadians, and the round figure 250,000 was often cited in newspapers and
speeches. When interpreted, these statistics meant that the French-
speaking portion of Ontario's population had increased from approxi-
mately 5 per cent of the total in the 1880's to nearly 10 per cent in
1910.[8]

For French Canadians in Ontario, knowledge of their increasing
strength provided fresh incentive for organization. Early efforts to
unite the French of Ontario met with little success. Around 1900 a
fleeting attempt was made but the conclusion reached was that "le
temps n'est pas venu."[9] In 1906 the Saint-Jean-Baptiste Society of
Ottawa formulated a detailed plan of federation but it was never
implemented.[10] Increasing numbers gave encouragement but the need
for concerted action had to be more fully demonstrated. An issue broad
enough and important enough to appeal to all French Canadians in
Ontario would be an invaluable aid. Such an issue was the education
of the French-speaking children.

In 1903 the arrangement agreed upon in 1886 which divided the
Ottawa Separate School Board into two sections, the French section
to control the management and finance of the French schools and the
English section to control the management and finance of the English
schools, was terminated and the two sections amalgamated to form
one administrative and financial unit. But the French Catholics and the
Irish Catholics did not work together peacefully for long. In 1904 the
French majority of the Board decided to build an elaborate school to
be conducted by the Christian Brothers principally in the French
language. Their plan was thwarted by an Irish Catholic named Grattan
who obtained a court injunction to prevent the Board hiring the
Christian Brothers as teachers. According to a clause in the Separate
School Act of 1863, "persons qualified by law as Teachers, either in
Upper or Lower Canada, shall be considered qualified Teachers for

[8]*Canadian Annual Review* (*C.A.R.*), 1911, p. 471. Margaret Prang, "Clerics, Politicians, and the Bilingual Schools Issue in Ontario, 1910–1917," *C.H.R.*, XLI (1960), 288.
[9]*Congrès d'Education des Canadiens-Français d'Ontario 1910, Rapport Officiel*
(Hawkesbury, 1909), p. 42 (hereafter *Congrès d'Education 1910*).
[10]*Ibid.*, p. 44.

the purposes of this Act." Thus, members of religious orders, exempt from examination in Quebec, might also teach as qualified teachers in the state-supported separate schools of Ontario. However, the Act had since been amended and it was now asserted that this clause applied only to persons who had been so qualified before Confederation. While litigation was proceeding, the English-speaking ratepayers, who although in a minority paid the greater share of the school taxes, demanded that the two separate sections of the Board be re-established as "the only solution to the present acute condition." Their demand was not granted but the Irish Catholics of Ottawa did win a significant victory in the court case. In November, 1906, the Judicial Committee of the Privy Council ruled that members of Quebec religious orders who joined after 1867 were not qualified to teach in Ontario without passing Ontario examinations.[11]

It was shortly after this court ruling that efforts to unite all French Canadians in Ontario began to attract more interest. Although the French-Canadian Congress of Education did not meet until January, 1910, the official report stresses that the Congress was no sudden occurrence, but rather the culmination of a long series of events and the result of very careful preparation. In March, 1907, T. Rochon, inspector of bilingual schools in eastern Ontario, organized a pedagogical convention which passed resolutions aimed at reforming the bilingual system and also appointed an impressive list of officers for the following year. The 1910 report credits this earlier convention with having awakened the slumbering spirit of Franco-Ontarians. If they could now be stimulated to action, a leader was readily available in Judge A. Constantineau, county judge of Prescott and Russell, who had been advocating a national congress for some time.[12]

However, the realization that unsatisfactory conditions exist does not necessarily result in any attempt at improvement. Since apathy is such a powerful deterrent to action, a sustained campaign to secure support was undertaken through the medium of the press. On September 11, 1908, in the little village of Hawkesbury in the county of Prescott, J. H. Laurin published the first number of a new weekly newspaper, Le Moniteur. Although modest in appearance and emanating from an obscure location, this newspaper undertook an important mission. Le Moniteur was dispatched to every French-Canadian home in the province to urge in forceful style: "Soyez unis, mettez de côté les intérêts des partis et en avant pour le triomphe de notre nationalité."

11C. B. Sissons, Church and State in Canadian Education (Toronto, 1959), pp. 82–4. Sissons, Bi-lingual Schools, pp. 71–2. C.A.R., 1914, p. 424.
12Congrès d'Education 1910, p. 46.

Each week it returned with the rallying cry, "L'union fait la force," so put aside lesser interests and join together to fight for French-Canadian rights in Ontario.[13]

The newspaper campaign was well in progress when Aurélien Bélanger, inspector of bilingual schools for Ottawa and surrounding district, called a meeting of school trustees and others interested in education. For those who had been advocating a French-Canadian congress, this small meeting, held in Ottawa on December 28, 1908, marked the transition from hope to actual preparation. When Inspector Bélanger asked the gathering what could be done to aid the separate schools, Curé Beausoleil replied, "Nous allons préparer un Congrès de tous les Canadiens-Français d'Ontario. Qu'en pensez-vous, mes amis?" After discussing various obstacles which might prevent success, those present decided to go ahead. Curé Beausoleil and Judge Constantineau were directed to invite the principal French Canadians of the area to a meeting to consider the proposal.

About a hundred leading French Canadians from the Ottawa district met on January 24, 1909, endorsed the project of a congress, and nominated a committee to communicate with the other groups of French Canadians in the province in order to secure their co-operation. These groups were canvassed by means of a circular letter which, among other questions, asked: "Quelles sont les conditions locales et vos besoins au point de vue de l'éducation?" From across the province came the quick and unanimous reply: "Venez à notre secours! . . . Sauvez nos écoles françaises!" At a meeting on May 4, 1909, the committee reported that province-wide support for a congress was assured, and therefore the detailed work of organization began. No aspect of preparation was ignored as seven committees—education, general interests, publicity, statistics, finance, organization, and reception—set to work. Soon all French Canadians in Ontario would be united by one organization and would be able to make the most effective use of their combined strength.[14]

It was primarily to defend French schools that the French-Canadian Congress was organized according to the official report of the Congress.[15] But what danger was threatening the French, or, more accurately, the English-French schools? Why did they need protection? Apart from an oblique reference to the loss of qualification by the Quebec religious orders, the report offers no explanation.[16] Certainly,

[13]*Ibid.*, pp. 47–9.

[14]*Ibid.*, pp. 52–92. This summary has been drawn solely from the 1910 Congress Report which provides a fairly full but rather disjointed account of the preparations. The report gives long lists of those who participated in the preparations but does not specifically indicate the principal organizers.

[15]*Ibid.*, p. 60.   [16]*Ibid.*, p. 52.

it was only after the Privy Council ruled against the religious orders that attempts to unite the French in Ontario received any real encouragement. But the court decision in itself would hardly seem a sufficient threat to evoke such a strong reaction. The sole effect of the ruling was to compel all religious teachers to obtain Ontario qualifications; in no way did it touch upon the use of French in the schools.[17] Why then the desperate appeal, "Save our French schools"?

The dispute in Ottawa which resulted in the Privy Council decision was only one skirmish in a long conflict between Irish and French Catholics. For Irish Catholics, the influx of French-speaking Catholics into Ontario had special significance. The school system of Ontario is established on the basis of religion, not of race. Consequently, Irish Catholics often found themselves forced into an uncomfortably close association with their French co-religionists. French-speaking children attended their schools; French-speaking trustees took their place on the separate school boards; even French-speaking teachers were hired to instruct the children. The friction inherent in the school situation was aggravated by a perpetual church feud which involved all levels of the Catholic clergy. Neither Irish nor French neglected any opportunity to strengthen their own position as they vied for control of the Catholic church in Canada. One prominent Irish Catholic of the time testified to the intensity of the conflict:

Now, no one wants to do the French Canadians an injustice. The British Crown has given them what is actually an empire in the Province of Quebec, but no right or claim have they on this account, or on any other, to all the Provinces of the Dominion. They have been, with difficulty, kept out of Church control completely, in Ontario and the Maritime Provinces; with difficulty driven out of that control in British Columbia. They are still in control of the Church organization in Manitoba, Alberta and Saskatchewan.[18]

In this struggle, French Catholics were steadily building up strength against Irish Catholics in eastern Ontario.

The clash was most severe in the city of Ottawa where the opposing forces met head on. Here, in the basilica whose stained-glass windows bore Irish names, services were now being conducted in the French language.[19] Here, too, the University of Ottawa provided a major battleground. The Oblate Order of France, which controlled the university for some time after it received its charter in 1866, made English the official language of the institution. Then, largely through

[17]There do not seem to be any statistics which show haw many teachers already employed were affected but the Ontario government made arrangements to enable these religious teachers to become qualified. University of Toronto Library, "Correspondence . . . concerning the Bi-lingual School Issue," Education Department Memorandum, 1907.

[18]Ontario, Department of Public Records and Archives, Whitney Papers, Father J. F. Coffey to Whitney, Oct. 27, 1910.   [19]*Toronto Daily Star*, Oct. 15, 1910.

the influence of Archbishop Duhamel of Ottawa, the Quebec Oblate Order with headquarters in Montreal gained control of the university and began converting it into a distinctively French institution. One important step in this process was the banishment to the United States of Father Michael Francis Fallon who had been vigorously opposing any increase in the use of French.[20] Fifteen years later, Bishop Fallon wrote: "My removal in 1898 as vice-rector of Ottawa university and my subsequent removal in 1901 as pastor of St. Joseph's church was the result of a deliberate conspiracy hatched in Montreal and Ottawa."[21] The French won the encounter at the University of Ottawa but strong personal motives for retaliation had been given to a man who was later to acquire much power as bishop of the diocese of London. In the meantime, the centre of attention shifted to the Separate School Board of Ottawa. The dispute which arose over teachers' qualifications was not the first incident of trouble between Irish and French and neither side expected that it would be the last. In a continuing conflict with aroused Irish Catholics, French Canadians of Ontario might well fear for the future of their schools.

At the same time, an important change occurred in provincial politics. After thirty-two years of power in Ontario, the Liberals suffered a crushing defeat in the 1905 elections. Conservatives led by the Hon. James Pliny Whitney swept the province, winning in 69 of the 98 constituencies.[22] The party traditionally supported by Orangemen now governed Ontario. The party which in 1890 demanded "English only" in all Ontario schools now controlled the school policy of the province. Could French Canadians in Ontario be blamed for feeling apprehensive? Three years later the Conservatives won an even more impressive victory. On June 8, 1908, Ontario voters elected 89 Conservatives, 16 Liberals, and 1 Independent to give the Conservatives the largest majority in the history of the province.[23] During its first term of office the Whitney government does not seem to have interfered in any way with the use of French in the schools. But shortly after the 1908 elections an important wing of the party began to show signs of discontent.

The Orange Order, dedicated to the preservation of Protestant supremacy and the imperial connection, saw in French-Canadian society the very antithesis of its most cherished values. In Quebec, ecclesiastical despotism had triumphed over the British ideal of individual liberty for all.[24] French-speaking Roman Catholics were

[20]*Toronto Daily Star*, Sept. 22, 1910; Whitney Papers, Father J. F. Coffey to Whitney, Oct. 27, 1910. [21]*Ottawa Citizen*, March 20, 1916.
[22]Province of Ontario, *Directory and Guide to Services of the Ontario Government* (Toronto, 1964), p. 263. [23]*Ibid.*, p. 264.
[24]*The Sentinel and Orange and Protestant Advocate*, Dec. 8, 1910.

vassals of the Church to an even greater extent than English-speaking Roman Catholics. According to the *Sentinel*: "English-speaking Roman Catholics are not so amenable to priestly influence as are the French. Association with Protestants has developed in them a larger (but still all too small) measure of independent action."[25] In addition, French Canadians were not linked by ties of language and tradition to the empire and their loyalty was questionable at best. Orangemen believed that the English language was one of the strongest bonds of imperial unity, and they viewed the extension of the French language into Ontario as a threat not only to British institutions but to the empire itself. In the opinion of the *Sentinel*, the dual language system was a vicious principle:

It is admirable to deal generously with the conquered race. But is it not fatal to grant them concessions which threaten the stability of our institutions? . . . There is another side to this question. . . . It is the ulterior purpose that is hidden as much as possible from public view. What is intended by the movement is to strike at the integrity of the Empire. Talk as we may about the loyalty of the French to Britain, the fact is patent to every observant man that Imperialism as it is understood in the English-speaking Provinces finds no favour among the French Nationalists. Independence is their goal.[26]

In the Orange Order's hopes and plans for Canada there was no room for French Canadians. Regrettably, the Canadian constitution had granted certain rights to French Canadians, particularly in Quebec, and these probably could not be rescinded. Under no circumstances, though, should these rights be extended. If the French Canadian came to Ontario he should accept Anglo-Saxon ideals: "He is welcome as long as he is willing to become one of us and co-operate in the upbuilding of an Anglo-Saxon community. If he has different ideals he had better go elsewhere. We cannot deny our past and do violence to our future in order to gratify his national ambitions."[27] However, French Canadians failed to recognize the superior worth of Anglo-Saxon traditions and determined to retain their own identity and customs. Confronted with the stubborn persistence of French Canadians, Orangemen felt both exasperated and alarmed. In the words of the *Sentinel*, "It is this refusal to assimilate that makes the French-Canadian so difficult to get along with."[28]

For the Orange Order, the increasing number of French Canadians in Ontario signalled danger ahead. Ontario, the stronghold of imperial loyalty and English Protestantism, was being taken over by the French. Orangemen had been reading *The Tragedy of Quebec* by Robert Sellar, editor of the Huntingdon *Gleaner* and a good Presbyterian.[29]

[25]*Ibid.*, Jan. 12, 1911. [26]*Ibid.*, April 7, 1910.
[27]*Ibid.*, Nov. 25, 1909. [28]*Ibid.*, Nov. 3, 1910.
[29]*Ibid.*, Dec. 9, 1909.

First published in 1907, the book describes with great poignancy and bitterness the expulsion of the English-speaking Protestant farmers from the Eastern Townships of Quebec. The parish system was the principal force driving out the Protestants but it received strong support from its close relation, the Catholic schools:

The text-books are Catholic, the whole atmosphere of the school is Catholic. The farmer cannot in conscience send his little ones to it, and so the French-Canadian, who has been wanting his farm, gets it, and a week after he is in possession a priest comes to see the new acquisition of his church, for it has joint proprietorship with the habitant in its acres. For the first time a priest drives up the lane lined by maples which the grandfather of the dispossessed Protestant planted, and levies tithes on the yield of fields his great-grand parents redeemed from the wilderness, and which four generations of Protestants have ploughed.[30]

Watching the influx of French Canadians from across the Ottawa and the establishment of more and more schools in which Roman Catholic catechism was taught and the French language spoken, Orangemen saw the tragic history of the Eastern Townships being re-enacted in the eastern counties of Ontario. Was even Ontario to be dominated by those twin evils, the Catholic hierarchy and the French language? The Orange Order answered with an emphatic: "No, not so long as it is within our power to prevent it!"

Early in 1909, D. Racine, the French-speaking member for Russell in the Ontario legislature, introduced a bill designed to give more funds to the separate schools, and the Orange Order's interest in the eastern counties increased.[31] The Joint Legislation Committee of the Order reported to the Grand Orange Lodges of Ontario East and West that school conditions in the eastern counties were far from satisfactory. Religious exercises were being conducted contrary to law and French was being used in the schools to the exclusion of English. After receiving this information, the Orangemen decided to send a special commissioner into the eastern counties to get statutory declarations concerning the conditions in the schools. They wanted to present an unassailable case against the schools and were willing to bear any expense involved.[32]

In the meantime, the Department of Education had not been idle. Dr. R. A. Pyne, the Minister of Education, had been making many changes in the school system in an attempt to improve standards generally. In the case of the English-French schools, this concern for educational progress was doubtless augmented by the fact that the government could not afford to ignore the obvious sentiments of the

[30]Robert Sellar, *The Tragedy of Quebec* (Huntingdon, P.Q., 1907), p. 200.
[31]*Ottawa Citizen*, March 12, 1909.   [32]*Sentinel*, Dec. 29, 1910.

Orange Order. On October 30, 1908, Dr. F. W. Merchant, Chief Inspector of Public and Separate Schools, was instructed to ascertain the general conditions and necessities of the English-French Schools in the Ottawa Valley.[33] In his confidential report submitted on January 9, 1909, Dr. Merchant informed the Department that the schools were predominantly French:

The atmosphere of the schools is undoubtedly French. The language of the teacher in conversing with the pupils or in giving general directions is French. The children use French in their ordinary conversations in the school and on the playground. The language of instruction in Forms I and II is almost exclusively French. In all but a few schools French is also used in teaching the subjects of Form III. Where a Fourth Form exists, the subjects of the entrance examination are usually taught in English but in three schools I found French used mainly in this grade.[34]

Although English was being taught in all schools, there was great diversity in the methods and the results. In general Dr. Merchant found that the pupils were not proficient in either English or French. However, he attributed most of the weaknesses in the English-French schools not to the system but to lack of training and experience in the teaching staffs.[35] He emphasized the need for training schools and recommended that the Ottawa bilingual model school be continued and placed on a more permanent basis and that a bilingual model school be established in the Nipissing district, preferably at Sturgeon Falls.[36]

Thus, at the beginning of 1909, both the Orange Order and the Department of Education were showing a growing concern for the state of the English-French schools of the province. This interest was not widely publicized; in fact, it was kept very quiet. Reports of Orange Lodge meetings in the spring of 1909 emphasize the separate school issue but do not mention the language question.[37] Until late 1909 the Orange *Sentinel* avoids any striking reference to the use of French in the schools. Dr. Merchant's report was filed as confidential and not released by the Department of Education. However, investigations of school conditions could never be completely concealed from those being investigated, especially since many of the schools concerned were located in the inspectorates of two bilingual inspectors, A. Bélanger and V. H. Gaboury. These two gentlemen, whom Dr. Merchant thanked for their assistance, participated actively in the preparations for the French-Canadian Congress.[38] Congress organizers would

[33]F. W. Merchant, *Report on English-French Schools in the Ottawa Valley* (Toronto, 1909), p. 1.
[34]*Ibid.*, p. 2.   [35]*Ibid.*, pp. 3–5.
[36]*Ibid.*, pp. 16–17.   [37]*C.A.R.*, 1909, p. 233.
[38]*Congrès d'Education 1910*, pp. 53, 57, 58, 66, 68.

probably have had no difficulty in obtaining a complete and official account of school investigations.

The continuing enmity between Irish and French Catholics, the activities of the Orange Order, and the investigations of the Department of Education can be used to construct a good case in defence of the French claim that action was needed to save their schools in Ontario. Yet fear doubtless magnified the existing danger. The agitation of the Orange Order was relatively subdued and the report of Dr. Merchant was, on the whole, sympathetic towards the French. In 1909 the Department followed Dr. Merchant's advice and established a new bilingual training school at Sturgeon Falls in an effort to provide better qualified teachers for the English-French schools of Northern Ontario.[39] But the French Canadians of Ontario, aware of their vulnerable position, were not inclined to trust the authorities. Dr. Merchant records the apprehension of a people whose existence was constantly threatened by a gradual assimilation process: "While there is practically no opposition to English, there is a very strong feeling, closely connected with racial, religious, and national sentiment that the French language must be maintained. Hesitancy in supporting the study of English is frequently the result of the fear that it will lead eventually to the suppression of French."[40]

Fear that French would be suppressed in the schools of Ontario was undoubtedly an impelling force in the organization of the French-Canadian Congress and the formation of the French-Canadian Education Association. But it was definitely not the only force. The French Canadians of Ontario were not simply responding to attack or to fear of attack; conscious of their increasing strength, they were taking the initiative. Their intention was not to *defend* their rights but to *extend* their rights, not only to protect existing rights but also to secure additional ones. A long editorial in *Le Moniteur* on September 10, 1909, outlined the purpose of the French-Canadian Congress: "The principal aim of this Congress is to obtain schools where the French language and religious instruction shall occupy a place of honour. For the execution of this design it is necessary for us to have primary bilingual schools, secondary bilingual schools, [normal] bilingual schools and as a crown to the whole a bilingual university."[41]

In addition, the Congress strove to secure public office for French Canadians in Ontario:

Considérant . . . que le chiffre de la population canadienne-française dans cette

---

[39]"Correspondence . . . concerning the Bi-lingual School Issue," Education Department Memorandum, 1915.

[40]Merchant's *Report on English-French Schools*, p. 8.

[41]Quoted in the *Sentinel*, Dec. 16, 1909.

province a *plus que doublé* dans les deux dernières décades, et que, malgré *cette grande augmentation*, ils n'ont encore qu'un seul sénateur et deux juges de comté, comme il y a quinze ou vingt ans . . . le Congrès d'Education des Canadiens-Français d'Ontario demande respectueusement et instamment la nomination d'un sénateur, d'un juge de la cour supérieure et de juges de la cour de comté, choisis parmi les Canadiens-Français de cette province.[42]

Was this the sort of programme which would be proposed by a group fearful that they were going to be deprived of their present rights? No, this was an ambitious nationalist programme, the product of racial consciousness and pride.[43] The enthusiasm shown for the movement to unite all the French Canadians of Ontario, whatever their occupation or political affiliation might be, was mainly the result of a very thorough and energetic campaign built up around the schools question.

Education was a vital issue in itself, for, as *Le Moniteur* pointed out, "L'avenir de notre race dans Ontario dépend de l'éducation que recevront les petits Canadiens-Français."[44] However, the educational issue might also be used for other purposes. Robert Rumilly in his *Histoire de la Province de Québec* suggests that there was another reason, a reason not publicly announced, for holding a Congress at this time: "Il s'agissait de défendre les droits scolaires. Il s'agissait bien aussi de faire une démonstration de nombre, d'union, de résolution, à l'heure où le clergé irlandais et le clergé canadien-français se contestaient la succession de Mgr. Duhamel."[45] The death of Archbishop Duhamel in 1909 left vacant the important archdiocese of Ottawa. The French clergy were most anxious to secure a worthy French successor to Archbishop Duhamel and a show of strength might be very effective against the claims of the Irish opposition. Members of the clergy took an active part in organizing the Congress; their subscriptions helped to defray the cost of the Congress, and many curés accompanied the delegates to Ottawa.[46] Of course, Catholic education is closely allied to the Catholic church, but it is not likely that the interest shown by the French clergy was entirely educational.

So, in response to a variety of forces, including educational problems, ethnic pride, religious strife, and directed by a few energetic leaders, the French Canadians of Ontario united. Over twelve hundred delegates from all parts of the province, all chosen by local nominating conventions, assembled in Ottawa on January 18, 1910, for the first

[42]*Congrès d'Education 1910*, pp. 264–6.

[43]A possible connection, either direct or indirect, between the movement to unite the French Canadians in Ontario and the Quebec Nationalist movement might be worth exploration.

[44]*Congrès d'Education 1910*, p. 47.

[45]Robert Rumilly, *Histoire de la Province de Québec*, XIV, 123–4.

[46]*Ibid.*, p. 123.

French-Canadian Congress of Education.[47] For three days they discussed their difficulties, their needs, and their hopes; they heard reports of various committees; they listened to speeches on education and general social interests. But the delegates took action as well. They founded a permanent organization called L'Association Canadienne-Française d'Education d'Ontario, with an executive committee composed of five officers, fifty members, and an impressive list of honorary members. Every person of French origin living in Ontario was made a member of the Association which had as its announced aim, "la juste revendication de tous les droits des Canadiens-Français d'Ontario et l'infatigable surveillance de leurs intérêts.[48] The statutes of the Association also provided for biennial conventions at which delegates from across the province would elect a new executive and decide on questions of general interest.[49]

In addition, the Congress unanimously adopted a series of resolutions to be presented to the Ontario government. The long preamble and fourteen resolutions essentially demanded that the French language be given a more official and prominent position in the elementary and secondary schools and in the teacher training institutions of the province. In connection with elementary education, the 1200 representatives of the French Canadians of Ontario urged that all schools where the majority of the pupils were French be declared English-French and in such schools French be authorized as a language of instruction and communication and a series of French readers and textbooks be approved; that instruction be given in French reading, spelling, grammar, composition, and literature in all schools where 25 per cent of the pupils were French; that the supervision of all such schools be given to bilingual inspectors; that French subjects be placed on the entrance examination and those writing the French subjects be allowed a lower passing grade in the English subjects. No mention was made of any desire to learn English; instead, the mistreatment of the Franco-Ontarians was emphasized: "There is in Ontario not a trace of secondary bilingual education with the result that the mass of French-Canadian children are forced to limit their studies to primary education, given under the most unfavourable conditions, and consequently popular instruction in the case of French-Canadians is maintained at an excessively low level."[50] Aggressive rather than conciliatory in tone, the document was not likely to win the sympathetic support of the government or of the majority of Ontario citizens.

---

[47]The official report lists the names of 1,245 delegates.
[48]*Congrès d'Education 1910*, p. 267.   [49]*Ibid.*, p. 269.
[50]Whitney Papers, Copy of Resolutions, Senator N. A. Belcourt to Whitney, Feb. 18, 1910.

The major decisions and discussions of the Congress took place behind closed doors. However, the display features of the Congress—the public reception at the Russell Theatre and the closing banquet at the Russell House—were just as important as the working sessions, for a public demonstration of unity and strength was one of the primary purposes of the Congress. At the Russell Theatre on the evening of January 19, a distinguished array of speakers addressed an audience of two thousand. Sir Wilfrid Laurier, Prime Minister of Canada; Rodolphe Lemieux and Charles Murphy, federal ministers; Frank Cochrane and Adam Beck, provincial ministers and official representatives of Sir James Whitney, headed the list of prominent political figures present, while the ecclesiastical dignitaries were led by Mgr. Routhier, administrator of the Diocese of Ottawa.[51] Although some speeches were made in French and some in English and although details varied, the point of each speech was virtually the same—praise for the French language and the French Canadians of Ontario. For this evening of eulogy, the keynote was struck by Sir Wilfrid Laurier: "La langue anglaise, c'est la langue des affaires, la langue française, c'est la langue de cœur. . . . Le Congrès doit poursuivre l'œuvre si bien commencée, travailler à *maintenir* et *améliorer* les écoles bilingues où les Canadiens-Français pourront apprendre et conserver, comme le plus précieux des trésors, leur belle langue française."[52]

The delegates would long remember this evening and it was intended that they should. The reception committee had worked hard to prepare "une fête dont le souvenir serait d'un puissant secours pour raviver dans les cœurs l'amour du nom canadien."[53] Now, representatives from all parts of the province, fortified by greater pride in their nationality and higher hopes for the success of their united efforts, would return home to transmit the new spirit to their neighbours. Such was the design of the Congress. The difficulty was that the Congress succeeded in rousing to action more than the French Canadians of Ontario.

The holding of a congress provoked an enemy who was already restless, and that enemy was not slow to retaliate. The Orange Order viewed the French-Canadian Congress as a challenge to Ontario, a challenge posed by a French-speaking invading army with big church and little school.[54] In the past, the French, and more particularly the French-speaking Catholic hierarchy, had moved cautiously and quietly in Ontario, but now they had come brazenly out into the open and declared their aspirations.[55] Orangemen welcomed this open challenge and responded to it by demanding that all bilingual schools in Ontario

[51]*Congrès d'Education 1910*, p. 215. [52]*Ibid.*, pp. 229–30.
[53]*Ibid.*, p. 90. [54]*Sentinel*, Jan. 6, 1910.
[55]*Ibid.*, Oct. 14, Dec. 9, 1909.

be abolished.[56] In December, 1909, the official organ of the Order, the *Sentinel*, began an educational campaign to acquaint the public with French aims in Ontario, and for some time thereafter devoted its attention almost exclusively to this cause:

Let there be no misconception of this French-Canadian Educational Congress on the part of the Protestants of Canada. Its avowed aim is the Gallicizing of the public and separate schools in Eastern Ontario. At present the teaching of the French language at all in these schools is simply a concession given by the ever-indulgent, broad-minded Protestant majority of Ontario. But the French-Canadians in Ontario, now numbering over 200,000, demand that this concession be glorified into a legal right.[57]

The *Sentinel* strenuously opposed the resolutions passed by the French-Canadian Congress:

It is part of the great ambition of the French that French be equal with English. Should that demand ever be conceded . . . the battle waged for a century will have been lost, and the barrier that Ontario has for so long opposed to the oncoming tide of French settlement will have been swept away. All that would mean to the destiny of Canada cannot readily be imagined. It would almost inevitably mean French domination and papal supremacy.[58]

However, the *Sentinel* was not too worried, for it was confident that the English-speaking citizens of Ontario, once aware of the danger, would soon rally to prevent French encroachment. Since the English were an overwhelming majority, any wise Ontario government would unhesitatingly turn down the impossible demands of the French Congress:

A blunt statement might serve to check the racial ambitions of our French fellow-citizens, and it would win the applause of English-speaking Catholics as well as of Protestants. There is little sense in alienating the French electorate by refusals so vague that Anglo-Saxon support is not rallied. Any set of politicians that cares to rely on the appreciation of the English-speaking people of Ontario, need be in no fear of the threats of any other race.[59]

Extreme and biased though many of the statements of the *Sentinel* were, there was nevertheless much truth in its contention that no Ontario government would grant the demands of the French Canadians if those demands were solidly opposed by the English-speaking population of Ontario. Therefore, it can be argued that, by holding a congress, the French Canadians seriously harmed their own cause. Before 1910 the Orange Order had shown considerable interest in the schools in the French-speaking areas of eastern Ontario, but it was the French-Canadian Congress which enraged the Orange Order and set off its vigorous public campaign against the French invasion of

[56]*Ibid.*, Nov. 25, 1910.   [57]*Ibid.*, Jan. 6, 1910.
[58]*Ibid.*, Feb. 3, 1910.   [59]*Ibid.*

Ontario.[60] By the late winter of 1910, thrust and counterthrust had become the order of the day. On February 9, 1910, a delegation of sixty prominent Orangemen representing the Grand Orange Lodges of Ontario East and West laid before Premier Whitney a series of 33 affidavits affirming that school laws concerning the use of French and the teaching of catechism were ignored and English-speaking school supporters unjustly treated in the eastern counties.[61] On February 18, 1910, a deputation from the French-Canadian Education Association, introduced by A. Aubin, M.L.A., presented their demands to the Premier and urged immediate action.[62] Whitney noncommittally promised both groups that he would give the subject thorough consideration. However, the Orangemen held the stronger position for, while they asked that existing school regulations be severely enforced, they did not at the moment ask for any change in the regulations. In addition, the Orangemen were more likely to secure support from the other English-speaking residents of Ontario than were the French Canadians.

Indeed, it was not long until another Ontario group stationed itself at the side of the Orange Order in firm opposition to French-Canadian demands. The Irish Catholics of Ontario certainly had little in common with the Orangemen, but they had their own good reasons for opposing French Catholics. Apart from the continuous church struggle, English-speaking Catholics feared that the French agitation would harm the separate school cause. During 1909 separate school supporters, led by the English-speaking Catholic bishops of Ontario, had been pressing the Whitney government to give them a larger share of the elementary school grants.[63] The hopes of the bishops and their followers were almost fulfilled early in 1910 when the government drafted plans for a re-apportionment of the school funds. But the plans never advanced beyond the drafting stage. On March 9, 1910, Whitney wrote to Archbishop McNeil of Toronto:

I regret very much that considerations beyond its control have prevented the Cabinet from giving proper and full consideration to the propositions laid before it by you some time ago. We fully expected to be in a position to do so before now, but the memorandum submitted to us on behalf of a Congress of French-Canadians held at Ottawa, has so complicated matters that we find it quite out of the question to deal with the subjects thoroughly during the stress of the sessions.[64]

---

[60]On Oct. 14, 1909, the *Sentinel* in an article entitled "A Challenge to Ontario," made its first attack on both the French-Canadian Congress and the bilingual schools.
[61]Toronto, *Mail and Empire*, Feb. 10, 1910. *Sentinel*, July 21, 1910.
[62]*Globe*, Feb. 19, 1910.
[63]"Correspondence . . . concerning the Bi-lingual School Issue," Folder 2.
[64]P.A.C., Landry Collection, Memorandum of Bishop Fallon for the Bishops of Ontario, Jan. 24, 1917, p. 9.

Shortly after they learned that all their efforts had been nullified by the actions of their French co-religionists, Irish Catholics gained a determined and energetic leader who had his own personal reasons for bitterness as well. On April 25, 1910, Michael Francis Fallon, the former Father Fallon of Ottawa University, was consecrated Bishop of London. The time for retaliation had come.

While in Sarnia on May 22, Bishop Fallon arranged a meeting with W. J. Hanna, member for West Lambton and Provincial Secretary in Whitney's cabinet. Most of the interview was devoted to the question of bilingual schools, a question which the Bishop personally regarded as dominating all other questions so far as the welfare of the people of his diocese was concerned. Mgr. Fallon used the occasion to serve notice that the Ontario government could count on his strenuous opposition if it ever succumbed to French-Canadian agitation. In the meantime he had determined, so far as it lay in his power, to wipe out every vestige of bilingual teaching in the public schools of his diocese; the interests of the children, some of whom had never learned to speak English, demanded that he take this course. Hanna was so impressed by the Bishop's earnestness that the following day he sent a complete written account of the interview to Dr. Pyne, with a copy to Premier Whitney. In Hanna's opinion: "His [Bishop Fallon's] whole attitude was not antagonistic by any means but there is no question about it he is a wonderfully strong character and is very much in earnest on this question and I could not but be impressed with the idea that on what may happen in this connection will turn his whole support or opposition throughout this Diocese."[65]

Other English-speaking Bishops of Ontario, and in particular Archbishop Gauthier of Kingston and Bishop Scollard of Sault Ste. Marie, viewed the creation of the French-Canadian Education Association as suspiciously as did Bishop Fallon.[66] In their interview on May 22, Bishop Fallon told Hanna that the French agitators aimed to control both church and state and that unless stamped out they would be as dominant in one as in the other. He then added that the majority of the bishops of the province had recently got together and put themselves on record and that shortly a deputation would call upon the government.[67] The deputation never appeared[68] and Bishop Fallon afterwards denied that the meeting had been held.[69] However, the English-speaking bishops did petition the government later in the summer. Meeting at Kingston on August 15, 1910, the bishops of the

[65]Whitney Papers, W. J. Hanna to R. A. Pyne, May 23, 1910.
[66]Memorandum of Bishop Fallon for the Bishops of Ontario, pp. 9–10.
[67]Whitney Papers, W. J. Hanna to R. A. Pyne, May 23, 1910.
[68]Sentinel, June 23, 1910.   [69]Globe, Oct. 17, 1910.

ecclesiastical provinces of Kingston and Toronto unanimously resolved:

That we are alarmed for the future of our Catholic educational system in Ontario because of the agitation that culminated in the French-Canadian Congress in Ottawa in January 1910; and that the Right Reverend the Bishop of London be delegated from this meeting to interview Sir James Whitney, Prime Minister of Ontario, and represent to him our entire opposition to the educational "Demands" of said Congress.[70]

Bishop Fallon later wrote that his interview with Premier Whitney on August 16 was "most satisfactory."[71]

With the beginning of a new school year in September, 1910, Bishop Fallon exercised his authority over the schools of his diocese. The Sisters of Saint Joseph at Belle River and at Walkerville were instructed to cease teaching French in their schools. At Windsor, the Sisters of the Holy Name, a French-Canadian order with its mother house in Quebec, were replaced by the Ursuline Sisters of Chatham, an Irish order.[72] The removal of the Sisters of the Holy Name also prevented the re-opening of a class to train bilingual teachers which the government had recently established at the convent. A Windsor separate school trustee later explained the change to Whitney:

His Lordship then forbade the sisters of the Holy Name to teach in our schools. As the Ecclesiastical head in the diocese he had to be obeyed and with regret the good sisters informed us of their inability to take charge of our schools in the face of the edict of His Lordship. We found ourselves powerless to resist the well laid plans of His Lordship and we had to take the Ursulines or close our schools. The teaching of French was then dropped in those schools and the class opened in the convent by the department was closed.[73]

While schools were opening without the use of the French language in Essex, the Twentieth Eucharistic Congress, the first ever held in North America, met at Montreal. Huge crowds and elaborate decorations greeted the high dignitaries of the Roman Catholic Church who assembled for a week of religious solemnity and splendour.[74] No church friction could penetrate such an impressive gathering—or so it seemed to the public at first. Then, on the evening of September 10, the scholarly Archbishop Bourne of Westminster startled an immense audience at Notre Dame Church by declaring that the Roman Catholic Church in Canada should identify itself with the English language

[70]Memorandum of Bishop Fallon for the Bishops of Ontario, p. 10.
[71]"Correspondence . . . concerning the Bi-lingual School Issue," Fallon to Pyne, Jan. 2, 1912.
[72]Landry Collection, Ecclesiastical Manuscript Pamphlet, "La Situation Religieuse des Catholiques-Français" (1912), Memoire No. 1, pp. 32–4; Resolution of French-Canadian Education Association, Ottawa Free Press, Oct. 14, 1910.
[73]Whitney Papers, Gaspard Pacaud to Whitney, Nov. 15, 1913.
[74]C.A.R., 1910, p. 351.

if it wished to advance. While most of the assembly listened with dismay or anger, Henri Bourassa hastily considered a reply. When his turn came, Bourassa discarded his prepared text and gave instead an impassioned defence of the French language. Bourassa's impromptu eloquence won for him the acclaim of his people. French Canadians in Quebec and across the country had found a strong champion to whom they could look for leadership and encouragement.[75]

Archbishop Bourne's speech and Bourassa's reply did much to inflame the language issue in Ontario. At the same time the newspaper announcement that Archbishop Gauthier of Kingston had been appointed head of the Ottawa diocese further incensed the French Canadians, for Archbishop Gauthier though French in name was Irish in mentality.[76] Therefore, almost immediately after the close of the Eucharistic Congress, the French-Canadian press set off in heated pursuit of Bishop Fallon, accusing him of having forbidden the use of French in the schools of his diocese. The publicity was probably much more extensive than the Bishop had anticipated. He responded by issuing a press statement on September 22 in which he emphatically denied that he had forbidden the use of French in the schools:

I have never been, by word or deed, by intent or desire, unfriendly to the interests of the French Canadian people and I never shall be unfriendly to them at any time or place no matter what the provocation. . . .

I have never issued, or caused to be issued, directly or indirectly, verbally, by writing, or in any other way, any order or mandate or even expression of opinion, concerning the teaching of French or any other language in the Separate Schools or in any other schools in the diocese of London, or any other place.

I have not, and I never have had, any objection to the teaching of French or any other language in accordance with the laws of the province of Ontario and the regulations of the provincial department of Education.[77]

Could Bishop Fallon's declaration be believed? The French-Canadian press thought not and published a document to substantiate their charges. This important document was a copy of the private letter which W. J. Hanna had written to his colleague, Dr. Pyne, the previous May giving a full account of his interview with Bishop Fallon. First printed in the *Revue Franco-Américaine* of Quebec on October 1, 1910, the letter was reprinted in *Le Devoir* on October 7, and from that point made the rounds of most Quebec and Ontario papers. Thousands of copies of a letter which was never intended for publication rolled off the presses. Soon all Ontario and Quebec knew that Bishop Fallon "had resolved, so far as it is in his power, to cause to

[75]Mason Wade, *The French Canadians* (Toronto, 1955), pp. 580–1.
[76]Landry Collection, Ecclesiastical Manuscript Pamphlet, "Rapport et Documents relatifs aux difficultés religieuses actuelles au Canada" (1917), p. 23.
[77]*Globe*, Sept. 23, 1910.

disappear every trace of bilingual teaching in the public schools of his diocese."[78]

The publication of this private and confidential letter lifted from the files of the Ontario government made sensational front page news. Interest was immediately attracted not only by the provocative nature of the letter but also by the intrigue which surrounded its disclosure. Shortly after the story hit the Toronto papers, Mr. Maisonville, private secretary to the Hon. Dr. Réaume, French-Canadian representative on Whitney's cabinet, accepted responsibility for the abduction of the letter and "resigned."[79] But the damage had already been done. Bishop Fallon announced that he was engaged in drawing up a reply which would act "considerably like a bomb,"[80] and on October 17 the promised bomb was featured in the newspapers. To an expectant province, Bishop Fallon declared that:

Not only was public education in certain sections of my diocese in a deplorable condition, but if any attention were to be given to the preposterous demands of the Ottawa French-Canadian congress it threatened to become more deplorable still. . . . Essex stands lowest educationally amongst the nine counties that constitute the diocese of London. Everything flourishes there except education. The land is heavy with rich harvests, choice fruits and a generation of uneducated children.

The whole statement was a ringing indictment of "an alleged bilingual school system which teaches neither English nor French, encourages incompetency, gives a prize to hypocrisy and breeds ignorance."[81]

Although Bishop Fallon might claim that he was opposed to the bilingual school system because it was grossly inefficient, the bilingual schools controversy which achieved such prominence in October, 1910, cannot be attributed solely or even primarily to a concern for high educational standards. The *type* rather than the *standard* of education was the centre of interest. The efforts of the French-Canadian Education Association were directed towards preserving and extending the rights of French Canadians in Ontario. For better or for worse the desire was that more French be legally taught in the schools, and any consideration of educational standards was purely incidental to the main purpose. The Orange Order made no pretence of concealing its motives. Bilingual schools should be abolished because they threatened the integrity of Anglo-Saxon institutions and would enable French Canadians to convert Ontario into another Quebec. Separate schools might have to be tolerated but not French schools! Bishop Fallon, as representing the Irish Catholics, expressed concern for the low standard of education in the bilingual schools but the remedy he prescribed was

[78]*Globe*, Oct. 13, 1910.
[80]*Star*, Oct. 13, 1910.
[79]*Star*, Oct. 15, 1910.
[81]*Globe*, Oct. 17, 1910.

not to improve the schools but to destroy them. The interests of the French-Canadian children, as interpreted by the Bishop, coincided rather well with the interests of Irish Catholics. It was these intense racial and religious forces which made the bilingual schools of Ontario an explosive public issue in 1910, and these same forces were to retain control, shaping the conflict that followed. In the mounting tension of the war years, the schism thus created made the Ontario bilingual schools issue an important national concern.

Clerics, Politicians, and the Bilingual Schools Issue in Ontario, 1910-1917

MARGARET PRANG

THE CONSERVATIVE VICTORY in the Ontario election of 1905 brought to power a party which had gone on record fifteen years earlier as opposing the use of any language but English in the schools of the province. During their years in opposition the Conservatives had made few criticisms of the regulations of 1890 which provided that French and German might be taught in districts where parents desired instruction in one of these languages, as long as English remained the language of general instruction. But a Conservative cabinet which included several Orangemen and a party which had a militant Orange wing might be expected to take a more active interest in the question. The most vigilant guardians of French-Canadian interests were now apprehensive.

They soon found cause for concern on February 25, 1906, when English-speaking separate school ratepayers in Ottawa passed a resolution calling for an end to the unified administration of the separate schools of the city, established only three years earlier, and a return to separate control of the finances and administration of the schools attended by the children of the two groups.[1] For the present, the English-speaking Catholics, who had recently become a minority in Ottawa, made no progress with their demands; however, at the end of 1909 they were cheered by the announcement that Father Michael Fallon, who had been a leading figure in the language controversy at the University of Ottawa and who had subsequently spent several

---

[1]C. B. Sissons, *Bilingual Schools in Canada* (Toronto, 1917), 72. For a concise outline of the language question in Ontario from pre-Confederation days see *Report of the Royal Commission on Education in Ontario,* 1950 (Toronto: The King's Printer), chap. XVI.

Reprinted from *Canadian Historical Review*, XLI (4), December, 1960

years in "exile" in the United States, was to return to Ontario as Bishop of London.

Bishop Fallon had been consecrated only some six months when much of the French-Canadian press began to accuse him of attempting to Anglicize the schools of his diocese by reducing or abolishing the teaching of French; Fallon denied that he wished to exterminate French from the schools but asserted that he favoured full obedience to a law which countenanced bilingual, but not French, schools.[2] Although determined to maintain the primacy of English in the schools, Bishop Fallon was anxious lest the school question explode in such a way as to make separate schools and the French language synonymous in the minds of the Protestant majority in the province. This catastrophe might well be precipitated by the majority's growing awareness of the rapid increase in the French-speaking population in Northern Ontario and the counties just west of the Ottawa River.

At the moment, separate school supporters could have no complaints against the Whitney government; early in 1910 the government began to draft plans for a redistribution of funds to the elementary schools, under which the separate schools would receive larger grants.[3] The proposed change naturally had the support of the bishops of the province,[4] and the English-speaking majority among their number hoped that agitation over the language question would not provoke hostility against separate schools in general so that the government would refuse to proceed with the redistribution. As a consequence of these fears the formation of the French-Canadian Education Association of Ontario in January, 1910, with its demand for "equal rights" for the French language in Ontario, created much tension between the French and English bishops.[5] Within two months of the Association's formation the fears of the English group proved justified when Premier Whitney informed the archbishops of the province that because of recent public agitation about the language question the government was unable to proceed with the plan for a redistribution of school funds.[6]

In the spring of 1910 when Bishop Fallon paid his first official visit to Sarnia, he invited the local member of the Legislature, W. J. Hanna, who was also Provincial Secretary, to call on him; to Hanna the bishop complained that in some schools in the county of Essex, which lay within his diocese, there were large numbers of pupils who were

[2]*Canadian Annual Review*, 1910, 421.

[3]University of Toronto Library. "Correspondence between the Ontario Department of Education and the Roman Catholic Authorities concerning the Bi-lingual School Issue," John Seath to Sir William Meredith, Feb. 17, 1910.

[4]*Ibid.*, G. F. Shepley to Sir William Meredith, March 10, 1910.

[5]*Ibid.*, memorandum of Bishop Fallon for the bishops of Ontario, Jan. 24, 1917.

[6]*Ibid.*, copy of Whitney to the archbishops of Ontario, March 9, 1910.

unable to speak English. The immediate cause of Fallon's alarm was the assertion by an English-speaking school inspector in Essex that he had received instructions from the Department of Education to cease inspecting certain bilingual schools, and his belief that a French-speaking inspector would be appointed in his place; further, Fallon had heard that the department was prepared to accept some Quebec teaching certificates in the Ottawa area. In short, it appeared to Fallon that the government was about to succumb to French-Canadian agitation; if his information proved correct he was prepared to wage total war against the government; meanwhile, he would do all he could to discourage the perpetuation of bilingual schools in his own diocese. Hanna, who seems to have been somewhat surprised and mystified by the intensity of Fallon's feelings, assured him that he was misinformed as to the government's intentions; then he sent a written account of the interview to Premier Whitney and to the Minister of Education, Dr. R. A. Pyne.[7] For the present Fallon made no public denunciation of what he understood to be government policy.

In mid-August the activities of the French-Canadian Education Association were the subject of heated discussions at a meeting of the bishops of the ecclesiastical provinces of Kingston and Toronto most of whom now believed that the whole position of separate schools was seriously threatened; they delegated Fallon to wait on Premier Whitney to request that there be no yielding by the government to the demands of the bilingualists; Fallon came away well satisfied that the premier had accepted his argument.[8] A month later the Twentieth Eucharistic Congress, the first such assembly held in North America, met in Montreal. This added to Protestant apprehensions (already aroused by the struggle over the application of the *Ne Temere* decree in Quebec) that the influence of the Roman Catholic hierarchy in Canada might be growing. The Eucharistic Congress did add fuel to the bilingual controversy when Archbishop Bourne of Westminster issued his unexpected call to the Canadian church to identify itself thoroughly with the English language if it would fully serve the Roman Catholic mission in Canada. This provoked an impromptu and impassioned reply from Henri Bourassa which immediately enhanced the nationalist leader's public influence and served notice on the rest of Canada that the fight for the French language throughout the Dominion would not be abandoned.[9]

It was against this background that G. Howard Ferguson, spokesman

[7]W. J. Hanna to R. A. Pyne, May 23, 1910, printed in full in Sissons, *Bilingual Schools*, 73–9.
[8]"Correspondence . . . concerning the Bi-lingual School Issue," Fallon to Pyne, Jan. 2, 1912.
[9]Robert Rumilly, *Henri Bourassa* (Montreal, 1953), chap. xviii, gives a colourful account of this episode and its effect in Quebec.

88   MARGARET PRANG

for the ultra-Protestant wing of the Ontario Conservatives, introduced in the Ontario Legislature in the spring of 1911 a motion asserting that "no language other than English should be used as a medium of instruction" in any school in Ontario.[10] For reasons which were probably not unconnected with the current efforts of the federal Conservative party to form the alliance with the Quebec Nationalists which was to prove so fruitful in the election later that year, Ferguson soon withdrew this resolution. He then introduced a modified resolution which declared that English should be "the language of instruction and of all communication with the pupils in the public and separate schools . . . except where, in the opinion of the department, it is impracticable by reason of the pupils not understanding English." This resolution received the unanimous support of both parties.[11]

In mid-October the unauthorized publication of W. J. Hanna's letter of eighteen months ago describing his interview with Fallon[12] caused the controversy to flare up again. The bishop exonerated Hanna from responsibility for publishing the letter, although he said that the document as published did not entirely accord with his own recollection of his conversation with Hanna; in particular, he asserted that the reference to a meeting of the bishops of Ontario had no basis in fact.[13] It appeared that Fallon was not averse to seeing the bilingual issue brought into the arena of full public debate; once this had happened his first contribution was a denunciation of the attempt of the Department of Education to carry on the study of both languages simultaneously, an approach which he believed pedagogically unsound, resulting in inadequate training in both languages and "encourag[ing] incompetency, giv[ing] a prize to hypocrisy, and breed[ing] ignorance."[14] Within a few days the government announced that Dr. F. W. Merchant, an official of the Ontario Department of Education had been appointed to investigate conditions in the bilingual schools.

With the question thus removed at least partially from politics for the moment, Whitney suddenly called an election for December 11. But the issue inevitably became an important one in the campaign although the newly elected leader of the Liberal party, N. W. Rowell, did not go out of his way to make it so, contenting himself in his initial address to the electors with a promise of "adequate training

[10]*Journals of the Legislative Assembly of Ontario*, March 22, 1911, 260.
[11]*Ibid.* This resolution was simply a confirmation of the existing law, Statutes of Ontario, 59 Vic. c. 70, s. 76.
[12]See note 7. The secretary of the French-speaking Minister of Public Works, Dr. J. O. Réaume, lost his position on charges that he had released the private letter for publication to a Quebec paper: Sissons, *Bilingual Schools*, 73.
[13]In two other documents Fallon says that the meeting was held. "Correspondence . . . concerning the Bi-lingual School Issue," Fallon to Pyne, Jan. 2, 1912 and memorandum of Bishop Fallon for the bishops of Ontario, Jan. 24, 1917.
[14]*Globe*, Oct. 18, 1911.

schools, a sufficient supply of competent teachers . . . to ensure under proper regulations that the pupils in every school . . . shall receive a thorough English education."[15] Rather, it was certain prominent members of the Conservative party and the Conservative papers, the Toronto *Telegram* and the *News*, who seemed most determined to keep the issue alive with their promises that they would oppose the teaching of any French in the schools.[16] But the Liberal *Toronto Daily Star* also helped to keep the issue before the public by publishing the results of investigations by two of its own reporters which showed that there were some areas of the province where French was used exclusively and that standards were generally low in the bilingual schools.[17]

As the election battle developed, it became increasingly clear that the language question cut across party lines. In the government ranks, the Attorney-General, J. J. Foy, a Roman Catholic of Irish origin representing the riding of Toronto South, declared for nothing but English,[18] thus allying himself with Bishop Fallon, Howard Ferguson, and the Orange Order. Foy's statement created anxiety among some Conservative politicians who predicted losses for the party in the coming election unless Premier Whitney publicly refuted Foy.[19] The statement of the Minister of Public Works, Dr. J. O. Réaume, a few days later, that, as a French-speaking Canadian he could confidently support Whitney's view that all children should learn English and might be allowed to use French in the early grades,[20] was apparently intended to undo any damage that might have been wrought by Foy.

Although the Liberals tried to use this display of cabinet dissension to show that the Conservatives had no policy, there was slight advantage in doing so, since they also exhibited a variety of convictions on the subject. While the recently retired Liberal leader, A. G. MacKay, member for the strongly Orange riding of Grey North, argued for no language but English,[21] Rowell told a North Bay audience that "the state has no right to say that these same children should grow up without further knowledge of the language which they first lisped at their mothers' knees."[22] Rowell's emphasis was somewhat less positive in the riding he was personally contesting, North Oxford; there, he stated that there was no excuse for schools where only French was

---

[15]Public Archives of Canada, Rowell Papers, *Address to the Electors by N. W. Rowell* (Ontario Reform Association, 1911).
[16]*Canadian Annual Review*, 1911, 473.
[17]*Toronto Daily Star*, especially issues of Nov. 20 and 22, 1911.
[18]*Globe*, Nov. 21, 1911.
[19]Ontario Archives, Whitney Papers, Andrew Broder to Whitney, Nov. 23, 1911; A. A. Aubin to Whitney, Nov. 28, 1911.
[20]*Globe*, Nov. 30, 1911.
[21]*Ibid.*, Dec. 1, 1911.
[22]*Ibid.*, Nov. 30, 1911.

taught and called on Whitney to declare whether he stood with Mr. Foy or Dr. Réaume.[23]

There were only two Ontario ridings, Prescott and Russell, in which French-Canadians were in the majority, but there were fourteen others in which they constituted 10 per cent or more of the population and possibly another six in which they might be decisive in a very close contest;[24] most of these were at present held by the Conservatives. When the election results came in two of the five seats gained by the Liberals were in ridings where the French-speaking vote was probably significant.[25]

In the first session of the new legislature, Rowell lost no time in raising the bilingual issue; in his first speech he observed that although the premier had said during the campaign that such schools did not exist in Ontario the public accounts provided for the salaries of three "inspectors of bilingual schools." Whitney refused to make any statement, pending the report of Dr. Merchant, but called attention to the resolution which had been approved unanimously in the previous session requiring English in all schools except where the students did not yet understand the language.[26] Rowell's further efforts to obtain a more specific statement of government policy were met by the well-founded charges of Napoleon Champagne, Conservative member for Ottawa East, that the Liberal leader was thoroughly equivocal in his own statements. Champagne declared that while Rowell had said that nobody should deprive a French-speaking child of his mother tongue, he had never spelled out just what this should mean for school policy. Rowell's reply can scarcely have satisfied Champagne; it asserted that the leader of the Opposition was under no necessity to declare a precise policy, and called attention again to the contradictory statements made by Conservative politicians in various parts of the province. In contrast, declared Rowell, the Liberal policy was consistent; every child must have "a thorough education in English . . . but we have no right to say any child shall be ignorant of its mother tongue."[27]

Toward the end of the session the controversy entered a new phase when the Merchant Report[28] was presented to the legislature on March 6. The report confirmed the charges of the critics of the bilingual schools; Dr. Merchant found that in 80 per cent of the separate schools

[23]*Weekly Sun* (Toronto), Dec. 6, 1911.
[24]The author's calculation, based on figures in *Census of Canada, 1911*.
[25]Party standings after the election were Conservatives, 83; Liberals, 22; Independent, 1; the Conservatives and Liberals each had three French-speaking members.
[26]*Globe*, Feb. 9, 1912.
[27]*Ibid.*, Feb. 21, 1912.
[28]F. W. Merchant, *Report on the Condition of English-French Schools in the Province of Ontario* (Toronto: King's Printer, 1912).

in eastern Ontario and in 90 per cent of the rural public and separate schools in the northern districts French was used in teaching all subjects except English, which was treated merely as one subject among others on the curriculum. The professional qualifications of most of the teachers in these schools were minimal and some had so slight a knowledge of English as to be doubtful teachers of the language. Thus, it was revealed that while there were some schools which might properly be called bilingual there were many more which were really French. Moreover, attendance at these schools was often poor and many children left school very early to go to work, equipped with an inadequate education in any language. Although Dr. Merchant admitted that the bilingual schools laboured under a difficulty not faced by others—the necessity of helping students to master a second language, English, in a short period of time—he could only conclude that "the English-French schools are, on the whole, lacking in efficiency."

Several attempts by the Liberals to secure an immediate debate on the report were rebuffed by government promises of a debate in due course. Finally, half an hour before prorogation, Whitney announced a school policy. The proposal provided for additional inspection of schools to assure testing of progress and enforcement of the regulations; henceforth, government grants to schools would be contingent on the employment of teachers able to instruct in English; no text books other than those authorized by the Department of Education were to be used; instruction in English was to begin as soon as a child entered any school; and, although French might be used as the language of instruction on the recommendation of the supervising inspector, this would not normally be continued beyond the first two years of school. Rowell asked whether the new policy meant that the regulations of the Mowat government, providing that French and German might be used fairly extensively in addition to English in specified areas, would be rescinded, and was told that they would not be withdrawn for the present. The opposition leader interpreted this to mean that, in practice, the use of French as a language of instruction was to continue pretty much as before; for this he thought there was "much to be said." Rowell also supported Dr. Merchant's recommendation that French be made a subject of study in public schools throughout the province, as it was in the high schools.[29] Thus, "Sir James had performed the sword dance awkwardly enough, but apparently without cutting his feet. Mr. Rowell had pirouetted on eggs without cracking a shell."[30]

[29]*Globe*, April 15, 1912.
[30]*World*, Toronto, April 15, 1912.

A few days later Rowell devoted most of an address at a Liberal rally in Toronto to the bilingual question. He accused the government of insincerity and cowardice and charged that the facts revealed in the Merchant Report had been known to the Department of Education for several years. He doubted whether the new provisions for inspection were adequate, but added that if the government pursued its announced policy the whole character of the bilingual schools would be improved.[31] The Liberal leader had, in effect, served notice that the government need fear no serious criticism from his party; there was now an essentially bipartisan policy on the bilingual schools.

The opponents of bilingual education felt confirmed in their views when the official census of 1911 was published. The census provided statistical proof that the racial division in Ontario in the second decade of the twentieth century was very different from what it had been in the days when Mowat had applied more generously regulations which were very similar to those announced by Whitney. Between 1881 and 1911 Ontario's population had increased from 1,926,922 to 2,523,274, a gain of nearly 600,000; in the same period the French-speaking population had increased from 102,743 to 202,442.[32] However, this latter figure was generally believed to be very conservative; the ecclesiastical census of the province in 1909 had reported 247,000 French-Canadians,[33] and the figure usually quoted by the politicians in 1911 was 250,000. Thus, in the preceding thirty-five years the French-Canadians had accounted for about 25 per cent of the total increase; where they had composed 5 per cent of the population in the 1880's they were now about 10 per cent. English-speaking alarmists found in the census support for such assertions as the one made, during the recent campaign by the Toronto *Star*, that in another twenty-five years Northern Ontario would have a population of two million, of whom 75 per cent would be exclusively French-speaking.[34] The prediction was hysterical, but it fed the fears of the majority in Protestant Ontario for whom

[31]*Globe*, April 20, 1912. The essential unity of the two parties on this issue is obviously due primarily to the dominantly English-speaking and Protestant character of Ontario, but in considering the reluctance of the opposition to criticize government policy it must be noted that at this time the Liberal party had a very powerful Protestant "directorate." Its leader, N. W. Rowell, was one of the most prominent Methodist laymen in the province; in the summer of 1912 a group of Toronto Liberals organized a fund to provide the leader with secretarial assistance and to place a party organizer in the field. This group included A. E. Ames, E. R. Wood, J. H. Gundy, W. E. Rundle, Col. F. H. Deacon, all leading financiers, and J. E. Atkinson, publisher of the *Toronto Star* and J. F. Mackay, business manager of the *Globe*. With the exception of Mackay, who was a Presbyterian, all of these men were active supporters of the Methodist church, and it is evident that they were frequently consulted on party policy.
[32]*Census of Canada, 1911*.
[33]*Canadian Annual Review*, 1911, 471.
[34]*Toronto Daily Star*, Nov. 30, 1911.

religion and language could not be separated; anyone could see that the bilingual schools were nearly all Roman Catholic separate schools. Nobody understood the possible implications of this identification more clearly than the Irish Catholic bishops.

Whitney's policy was formalized on June 15, 1912, when the Department of Education published a new circular of instructions on the bilingual schools, soon popularly known as "Regulation 17."[35] Ten days later in Quebec City the first French Language Congress held in North America pronounced itself firmly in favour of the extension of fully bilingual schools to every province where there were numbers of French Canadians.[36] This aspiration was supported on the platform of the Congress by a member of Whitney's cabinet, Dr. Réaume.[37] Before the opening of the new school term the government issued a further order, "Regulation 18." It ruled that any school which failed to comply with Regulation 17 would forfeit support from public funds and that its teachers would be liable to suspension or cancellation of their certificates.[38] These measures received enthusiastic endorsement by the Irish Catholic clergy of the province who urged Whitney to stand firm in his clear distinction between separate and bilingual schools.[39] At the same time Conservative politicians in Ottawa and Quebec were alarmed at the damage which they believed Whitney's policy would do to the party's prospects in Quebec.[40] Prime Minister Borden commented on "the very great outcry in the Province of Quebec" and requested Whitney to give "a reliable and correct statement of the regulations and the reasons why the same were promulgated . . . to

[35]The most controversial parts of Regulation 17 were in Section 3: "(1) Where necessary in the case of French-speaking pupils, French may be used as the language of instruction and communication; but such use of French shall not be continued beyond Form I, excepting during the school year of 1912–13, when it may also be used as the language of instruction and communication in the case of pupils beyond Form I who, owing to previous defective training, are unable to speak and understand the English language. (2) In the case of French-speaking pupils who are unable to speak the English language well enough for the purposes of instruction and communication, the following provision is hereby made: (a) As soon as the pupil enters the school he shall begin the study and use of the English language (b) As soon as the pupil has acquired sufficient facility in the use of the English language he shall take up in that language the course of study as prescribed for the Public and Separate Schools." The regulation is published in full in Sissons, Bilingual Schools, Appendix 2; also in Report of the Minister of Education, 1912 (Toronto: King's Printer, 1913), 211–13.
[36]Robert Rumilly, Histoire de la Province de Québec (32 vols., Montreal, 1940–60), XVII, chap. iv.
[37]Globe, June 25, 1912.
[38]Report of the Minister of Education, 1912, 213–15.
[39]Whitney Papers, Bishop D. J. Scollard to Whitney, Oct. 21, 1912; Bishop W. A. Macdonell to Whitney, Nov. 13, 1912; Very Rev. A. E. Burke, president of the Catholic Church Extension Society, to Whitney, Nov. 14, 1912.
[40]Ibid., Thomas Chapais to Whitney, Oct. 10, 1912; L. P. Pelletier to Whitney, Oct. 21, 1912.

some of our friends in Quebec . . . because misapprehension as to the course your government has pursued is likely to do mischief."[41] Whitney's reply was merely a digest of the Merchant Report. He asserted that the new regulations were designed simply to enforce a policy which had been in effect for many years but which, of late, had not been properly administered; no injustice was being done to anyone and he was confident that the majority of French-Canadian parents in Ontario wanted their children to learn English and were satisfied that this would not rob them of their French language and heritage.[42]

Opposition within the province came to a focus at the end of the year when a large delegation representing nearly all the French-speaking school districts waited on Whitney to demand the withdrawal of Regulation 17. The delegates argued that the ruling was not only unjust and illiberal but also *ultra vires* because it was contrary to the earlier Regulation 12 which still permitted both French and German in some schools. In defending his policy the premier asked "where in any country . . . an hour a day was allowed in each class for the study of one subject" as was allowed for French in Ontario. He found that nobody could mention so generous a provision elsewhere.[43] He then assured the protesters that every inspector would report at the end of the current school year on the effects of the instructions now being followed and might recommend changes, but he allowed none of his audience to entertain the slightest hope that a third type of school, "the racial school," would be tolerated.[44] Many Irish Catholics were now confident that the whole issue was settled and that little more would be heard of it.[45]

Certainly the Liberal party in Ontario, having once given tacit approval to Regulation 17, showed no disposition to discuss the subject. In spite of earlier appeals from some English-speaking Catholic Liberals that the federal Liberal party should publicly disavow the activities of Senator Belcourt and other Liberals in the French-Canadian Education Association of Ontario,[46] Laurier had thus far made no public comment. When Laurier appeared on the platform in Toronto in October, 1912, with Rowell, Sir Allen Aylesworth, and Sir George Ross, who had been Minister of Education under Mowat, there was no

[41]*Ibid.*, Borden to Whitney, Oct. 16, 1912.
[42]*Ibid.*, Whitney to Thomas Chapais, Oct. 16, 1912; Whitney to Borden, Oct. 17, 1912; Whitney to L. P. Pelletier, Oct. 22, 1912.
[43]*Ibid.*, Whitney to Archbishop C. H. Gauthier, Dec. 28, 1912.
[44]*Globe*, Dec. 28, 1912.
[45]Whitney Papers, Fallon to Whitney, Dec. 28, 1912; Michael O'Brien, inspector of separate schools, Peterborough, to Whitney, Dec. 28, 1912; Whitney to S. M. Genest, Jan. 9, 1913.
[46]P.A.C., Laurier Papers, Fallon to Charles Murphy, June 3, 1911; Murphy to Laurier, June 19, 199.

reference to the language question. Throughout the autumn Rowell and other Ontario Liberals kept clear of the issue in their prepared addresses. When he was asked a direct question, Rowell's answer was always that he favoured an adequate English education for every child; beyond that he would not go. Laurier's public advice to French-Canadians in Ontario "to speak French at home and English on the street"[47] was understood in some Conservative circles at least to mean that federal Liberal leaders had no serious objections to Ontario's policy.[48]

During the 1913 session of the legislature the only reference to the bilingual issue came from two French-speaking Liberals, Z. Mageau and Gustave Evanturel of the constituencies of Sturgeon Falls and Prescott. They demanded the publication of letters from Bishop Fallon to members of the government since 1910, and, charging that Dr. Réaume's continued presence in the cabinet constituted a betrayal of his race, they called for his resignation. No English-speaking Liberals supported their two colleagues, the government refused to be drawn into battle,[49] and to the evident relief of both parties the session ended without any major discussion.

In the following August the government issued Regulation 17 in a slightly revised form. The Chief Inspector was given power to permit the use of French as the language of communication beyond the first two years of study where he deemed it necessary, and to allow the study of French for more than one hour a day in certain schools, provided he was satisfied that this would not retard the pupils' progress in learning English.[50] Thus, while the objective of the policy remained unchanged, the rules could be applied more leniently at the discretion of the Department of Education. Although the Minister of Education denied charges that this represented a partial retreat from the original policy,[51] the government was chastised by the Conservative *Mail and Empire* for its weakness.[52]

Meanwhile, during the autumn of 1913 meetings of the Saint-Jean-Baptiste Societies in Quebec were better attended than they had been in many years and the dominant theme was always the fate of the beleaguered brethren in Ontario. The fifth annual convention of the French-Canadian Education Association enjoyed the largest registration yet, and during its sessions unremitting war against Regulation 17

[47]*Ottawa Journal*, Nov. 20, 1912.
[48]Whitney Papers, J. A. Ellis to Whitney, Nov. 27, 1912; Whitney to Ellis, Nov. 29, 1912.
[49]*Globe*, Feb. 8 and March 4, 1913.
[50]*Report of the Minister of Education, 1913* (Toronto: King's Printer, 1914), 318–20.
[51]*Globe*, Sept. 19, 1913.
[52]*Mail and Empire*, Sept. 19, 1913.

was again declared. A few weeks later Henri Bourassa carried his campaign against the regulation into Ontario itself where he delivered a number of addresses.[53] In Ottawa, Roman Catholics who sent their children to public schools to ensure that they were taught in English were threatened with refusal of the sacraments,[54] while the provincial government announced that the Ottawa Separate School Board would receive no public funds, since it had refused to submit reports on its affairs or to admit inspectors during the past year.[55]

During a by-election in Peel when the Provincial Treasurer, I. B. Lucas, challenged the Liberal leader to state his school policy in concrete terms, Rowell was forced into breaking his silence. After noting that the French Canadians were playing an important part in the development of the province and now constituted one-tenth of the population, Rowell chastised the government for the neglect which had produced the conditions revealed in the Merchant Report, rehearsed the conflicting statements of cabinet members on the bilingual issue, and asserted that it was little wonder, in view of Whitney's promises to stand by the original rules, that the Conservative press and the Orange Lodges felt betrayed by the revised Regulation 17; on the other hand, the French Canadians also felt that they were the victims of bad faith. Once more, in contrast to the government's vacillation, the Liberal policy was firm: "What we are concerned about is that they [the pupils] should master English and not that they should be ignorant of French. The problem in its working out is largely one of teachers and administration." There was still no direct comment on Regulation 17 or its revised form.[56]

In the 1914 session of the legislature both parties again ignored the bilingual question. When the ailing Whitney suddenly called an election for June, 1914, the Liberals tried to keep their "abolish-the-bar" programme as the central issue, and to avoid the language question; but the Conservatives, while campaigning primarily on their record in promoting the economic development of the province in the last nine years, seemed less anxious to by-pass it.[57] In any case, in view of the great public interest in recent events in Ottawa, it could scarcely be ignored completely. There, the English and French members of the Separate School Board were at loggerheads over the latter's refusal to

[53]For an account of French-Canadian reaction to Regulation 17 see Rumilly, *Histoire*, XVII–XXII, *passim*.
[54]*Mail and Empire*, Sept. 1, 1913.
[55]*Ibid.*, Oct. 24, 1913.
[56]Rowell Papers, MS of address, Oct. 27, 1913.
[57]Rowell told Laurier later that in this election the government had used the bilingual question to divert attention from "abolish-the-bar." Laurier Papers, Rowell to Laurier, April 15, 1916.

enforce Regulation 17. When the French-speaking section sought a city by-law allowing it to issue debentures to raise money for new schools to be operated independently of the Department of Education's language rulings, the English minority obtained a court injunction preventing this move and called on the government to enforce Regulation 17 or to withdraw it. On the eve of the election the Supreme Court of Ontario was beginning hearings on the validity of the injunction.

During the campaign the government renewed its pledges of full enforcement of Regulation 17, while the Liberals continued to assert that there could be no objection to the study of French in the schools as long as children learned English but declined to say what they would do with Regulation 17 if elected. W. R. Plewman, who had recently resigned as editor of the Orange paper, the *Sentinel*, because of the Conservative "betrayal" in revising Regulation 17, urged the election of the Liberals as the means of safeguarding the English language.[58] At the same time the Ottawa paper, *Le Droit*, founded in 1913 for the specific purpose of defending French interests in Ontario, advised its readers to support the Liberals as the guardians of the French language.[59]

At the end of June the Conservatives were swept back into power with a slightly larger popular vote than they had received in 1911, but the Liberals gained six seats including three of the six newly created seats and two previously held by French-speaking Conservatives: one of these was Essex North, where Dr. Réaume was defeated, the other Ottawa East. In the new legislature there were thus six French-speaking members, five Liberals and one Conservative, as compared with three of each in the previous House.

The day after the Ontario provincial election the Ottawa Separate School Board closed all its schools, asserting that since it had been deprived of some of its provincial grants it could not pay its teachers. The chairman of the Board soon admitted that the purpose of this action was to force the Department of Education to consent to the Board's employment of twenty-three Christian Brothers whose teaching certificates were not valid in Ontario. Thus, with the opening of the school term in September, 1914, some 8,000 Ottawa students were without teachers. The Ontario Supreme Court ordered the Board to reopen the schools and to employ only qualified teachers. This court ruling was the signal for renewed protests from French-Canadian leaders. In Montreal on December 21 party ties were forgotten as Nationalists Henri Bourassa and Armand Lavergne, the Conservative

58*Canadian Annual Review*, 1914, 448.
59*Ibid.*, 454.

Senator Landry, and Liberal Senators Dandurand and Belcourt appeared on the platform with Archbishop Bruchési and other church dignitaries to launch a campaign to raise funds for "les blessés d'Ontario."[60] Early in January, 1915, Cardinal Bégin published a letter to Archbishop Bruchési defending the inalienable right of every race to its own language and affirming the "noble duty of the French and Catholic province of Quebec to assist with all its influence and all its resources those who suffer and struggle until full justice shall be rendered them."[61] Within a week the Quebec legislature had adopted unanimously a resolution deploring the controversy and asserting that the legislators of Ontario were deficient in their understanding and application of traditional British principles.[62]

The increasingly active participation of the Quebec clergy in the protest movement naturally confirmed Ontario Protestants in their conviction that extension of the French language inevitably meant extension of the power of the Roman Catholic Church. However, Father Michael Whalen of Ottawa soon gave a demonstration that his church did not possess the monolithic character usually ascribed to it by Protestants. He published an open letter to Cardinal Bégin blaming the racial war on *Le Droit* and on extremists in both political and clerical circles:

We can easily explain why continuous reckless raiding on the schools of the province, to make them French, was regarded by the Protestant majority as a carefully planned campaign by the Quebec hierarchy to acquire on Ontario soil dominion in civil affairs. We deny that the French-Canadian raiders on the school system of Ontario have a right to declare, in the name of the Catholic Church, a religious war on the Government of this province. We protest against their dragging religion into their language agitation; we protest against their identifying their cause with that of the Separate Schools; we reprobate their methods as un-Catholic. We assert that only the united Catholic Hierachy of Ontario has a right to declare a Province-wide religious war against a law or regulation of the Ontario government. The United hierarchy has not done so.[63]

After revealing in the 1915 session of the legislature that 190 bilingual schools had ceased to be eligible for grants of public funds during the past year because of their failure to conform to the language regulations,[64] the government secured passage of a bill empowering it to set up a commission to take over the duties of the Ottawa Separate School Board if that body continued to defy the Department of Education. During the debate on this measure most of the English-speaking

[60]Rumilly, *Histoire*, XIX, 104.
[61]*Globe*, Jan. 9, 1915.
[62]*Ibid.*, Jan. 15, 1915.
[63]*Mail and Empire*, Feb. 14, 1915.
[64]*Globe*, March 26, 1915.

Liberals refrained from taking any part, but they voted for the bill.[65] Toward the end of the school term the government announced that it was paying the overdue salaries of qualified teachers in the inspected English separate schools of Ottawa directly to the teachers in order to keep these schools open.[66] Shortly after this, the Ottawa Board's appeal against the earlier court order to reopen the schools was rejected.[67] A week later an Order-in-Council placed the Ottawa separate schools under the jurisdiction of a three-member commission, and in the autumn of 1915 the Supreme Court of Ontario sustained the validity of Regulation 17. Chief Justice Sir William Meredith said he could find no support whatever for the view that the French language was guaranteed either by constitutional or natural right.[68] With every round won by the Ontario government, French-Canadian resistance stiffened.

The issue was now complicated by open expressions of English-Canadian suspicions that French Canada was providing considerably less than its share of army recruits, and by French-Canadian retorts that when justice was done in Ontario it would be time to talk about the war in Europe. At the third biennial congress of the French-Canadian Educational Association of Canada Bishop Latulippe of Temiskaming claimed that his recent presentation of the claims of the Franco-Ontarians had received the entire support of the Pope. Encouraging reports were also presented showing the receipt of funds from even the remotest Quebec villages for the war on the Ontario front.[69] Two weeks later the Quebec legislature bolstered this cause by passing a bill allowing local Catholic school commissions to contribute officially to the fund.[70]

The Quebec legislature's action was greeted with much strong language, especially from the Conservative press of Ontario, and the Liberal *Globe*, in the strongest editorial it had yet published on the subject, now asserted that Regulation 17 was fully justified and denounced much of the French-Canadian press for its unfounded contention that the French language in Ontario had a legal status which must be defended.[71] For the first time Laurier was brought into sharp conflict on this issue with the leaders of Ontario Liberalism. Laurier accused the *Globe's* editor, Stewart Lyon, of deserting traditional Liberal policy; what was needed was an enforcement of the Mowat policy, which would rightly rule out the existence of exclusively French

[65]*Ibid.*, April 2, 1915.
[66]*Ibid.*, June 4, 1915.
[67]32 Ont. L.R. 245.
[68]34 Ont. L.R. 335.
[69]Rumilly, *Histoire*, XXI, 45.
[70]*Ibid.*, 48–52.
[71]*Globe*, Feb. 26, 1916.

schools, but would allow for the learning of French as well as English by those who wished to do so. "Instead of this, Regulation 17 . . . practically wipes out the teaching of French. . . . This is a very serious matter . . . which must be considered immediately if I am to remain in the position which I now occupy."[72] At the same time Rowell complained to Laurier about the intervention of Quebec in the affairs of Ontario through its authorization of "a fund to carry on bilingual agitation in Ontario," and declared that it was essential that he make a statement in the legislature making clear the position of the Ontario Liberal party—that "the question is one which must be settled by the people of Ontario alone." As it was now five years since the Merchant investigation he would propose a new one to see how Regulation 17 had worked out in practice, and whether in fact any French-Canadian children were being deprived of a knowledge of French. He suggested that a three-member commission composed of the Roman Catholic Archbishop, Neil McNeil of Toronto, a representative of the Ontario French-Canadians, and some independent person of the prestige of President Falconer of the University of Toronto should examine present conditions and make recommendations for future policy. Any suggestions Laurier could make about further steps which Rowell might take to improve relations between Ontario and Quebec would be heard gladly, as long as Laurier remembered Rowell's basic position:

I cannot depart from the position I have always taken . . . that it is the duty of the state to see that every child in the Province receives a good English education and that consistent with this requirement, where the parents of the children desire that the children should also study the French language, there should be no objection to their doing so. The practical difficulty is to ensure the first without appearing unduly to interfere with the second, and the difficulty is greatly increased by the extravagant and entirely unwarranted claim put forth by the Nationalists with reference to the right to use the French language in this province.[73]

Laurier said he agreed with Rowell's general statement of policy, but added: "I would express it, however, more strongly than you do, and I would substitute for the words, 'there should be no objection to their doing so,' that 'the law should provide that they may do so.'" He welcomed Rowell's proposed commission, thought Archbishop McNeil an excellent choice, and as the French-Canadian suggested Bishop Latulippe whose extreme views represented a position which must be considered. Laurier thought Rowell's interpretation of the recent action of the Quebec legislature was probably unfounded, but said he would look into it: "I would be much surprised if a man of Gouin's prudence

[72]Laurier Papers, Laurier to Stewart Lyon, Feb. 29, 1916.
[73]Ibid., Rowell to Laurier, Feb. 29, 1916.

had allowed the passing of a law to carry on bilingual agitation . . . but what I believe is that the Legislature has authorized municipalities to assist French children in Ontario in obtaining a French education in addition to the English education." Laurier found the Ontario Department of Education "much confused not only in their ideas but in their language," but after studying the rulings he believed he understood their meaning:

. . . the French language can be taught with certain restrictions in all schools where it was taught in the month of August, 1913, but is not to be taught in any other school, that is to say, that henceforth the Orange doctrine is to prevail—that the English language only is to be taught in the schools. That seems to me absolutely tyrannical.[74]

The extent of anxiety among Quebec Liberals about the meaning of the term "hitherto" in the regulation was further revealed when Stewart Lyon held consultations with Laurier, Senator Dandurand, and Rodolphe Lemieux; they interpreted it as prohibiting French entirely in new schools established after August, 1913.[75] Lyon was commissioned to find out what it meant in Rowell's mind. He received an answer which implied that their understanding was probably correct:

He is inclined to take the view that it does not limit the teaching of French after the first form or the second form at the option of the inspectors in a greater degree than the Legislature intended. An amendment, however, except as part of a general settlement, could not be put through the Legislature at the present time. Howard Ferguson and the extreme Orange element feel that there is Party advantage for them in insisting upon greater restrictions in the teaching of French, just as Bourassa, Lavergne and the extreme partisans on the other side feel that there is advantage for them in insisting upon the recognition of French as an official language in the Province of Ontario.[76]

Meanwhile, Rowell's conversations with Archbishop McNeil, who was now making overtures to the Franco-Ontarian bishops to ascertain their terms for a settlement, left him with the conviction that "if McNeil once went into the case his shrewd common sense and absence of bias . . . would be an important factor in settling the dispute." However, he was less hopeful that Premier Hearst would respond to his

[74]Ibid., Laurier to Rowell, March 1, 1916. This letter is printed in O. D. Skelton, Life and Letters of Sir Wilfrid Laurier (2 vols., Toronto, 1922), II, 475.
[75]The disputed word appeared in Section 4: "In schools where French has hitherto been a subject of study, the Public or the Separate School Board . . . may provide, under the following conditions, for instruction in French Reading, Grammar, and Composition in Forms I to IV . . . in addition to the subjects prescribed for the Public and Separate Schools." The regulation clearly allows the interpretation given it by Laurier. However, in expanding the discretionary powers of the department, the revised form of 1913, allowed the minister to designate certain schools so that they would come under the old Regulation 12. See Sissons, Bilingual Schools, 108–12.
[76]Laurier Papers, Lyon to Laurier, March 6, 1916.

plan for a fresh investigation of the bilingual schools unless consider-able pressure were brought to bear upon him by federal Conserva-tives.[77] Yet some modification of Conservative policy seemed possible for Laurier was waited upon by an unofficial emissary from Hearst and Borden with the information that the Ontario government was disposed to make a compromise with the Ottawa Separate School Board and agree that if the schools were reopened the government would pay the teachers. Regulation 17 would then remain in abeyance until its validity was determined by the Judicial Committee of the Privy Council. However, said the Conservative spokesman, Hearst was afraid to go ahead with this compromise for fear of attack from the Liberals. Laurier's assurance that Rowell would "consider the matter fairly and even sympathetically"[78] was met by the Ontario leader's willingness to discuss the matter, although he made no comment on the general nature of the proposed compromise.[79] There is no evidence that any overtures were actually made to Rowell, and it must be concluded either that the Ferguson wing of the party refused to have anything to do with a compromise, or that apprehension about the Liberal reaction to such a plan remained sufficiently strong to prevent the move.

The case for a truce was shortly put forward very strongly by rep-resentatives of the Montreal Chamber of Commerce who conferred in Toronto with politicians and business leaders of both parties with a view to securing a relaxation in the enforcement of Regulation 17 until the end of the war or the Privy Council decision on its status. This move was dictated by a mixture of patriotism and commercial interest since Montreal firms owned by English-speaking Canadians were find-ing their goods boycotted by their French-Canadian customers and many Toronto firms had been told by Quebec clients that until On-tario did justice to the French language they would place no further orders.[80]

Within a week of the Montrealers' trip Rowell introduced in the legislature his plan for a three-man commission to examine the opera-tion of Regulation 17 during the past five years. At the same time he reaffirmed Ontario's absolute right to control education without out-side interference. The government, speaking through the Acting Minister of Education, Howard Ferguson, claimed that it understood the situation well enough without setting up another commission and nothing came of Rowell's proposal. He can scarcely have expected any other result; the delay occasioned by another investigation might have

[77]*Ibid.*
[78]*Ibid.*, Laurier to Rowell, March 4, 1916.
[79]*Ibid.*, Rowell to Laurier, March 7, 1916.
[80]*Ibid.*, M. K. Cowan to Laurier, April 12, 1916.

reduced tension within the federal Liberal party and made life easier
for certain Montreal and Toronto business interests, but it would undoubtedly have been interpreted by many Ontarians, probably by a
majority, as capitulation to Quebec. Given this public temper there
was no political necessity for the Ontario government to give even the
appearance of being willing to reconsider its policy; indeed, all the
political arguments pointed in the opposite direction. By the same
token the assurance that the government would reject a further commission made it safe for the Liberals to propose one without too much
political risk to themselves; and possibly the gesture would be worth
something in relations with the Quebec Liberals in the federal party.
In short, there could be no disagreement with the comment of one of
Laurier's closest friends in Ontario who declared that public opinion
was almost entirely in favour of the strict enforcement of Regulation
17 and would "oppose and slaughter any man or any party who talks
of granting greater privileges to the French."[81]

While Ontario maintained this near unanimity there were pressures
within both federal parties to take a positive stand in the controversy. Borden refused the request of the three Quebec members of his
cabinet that the Dominion government refer the whole question of the
status of the French language in Canada to the Privy Council,[82] on the
ground that under Section 133 of the B.N.A. Act the issue was already
settled.[83] Borden also rejected Senator Landry's suggestion that a government supporter should sponsor a motion of censure of Ontario's
policy in the House of Commons,[84] as well as the more desperate
remedy sought in a petition signed by Landry, Cardinal Bégin, and
most of the French-Canadian bishops—federal disallowance of Regulation 17.[85] As far as short-term political strategy was concerned it was
easy enough for Borden to resist these demands. The presence of the
three Quebec members in his cabinet was a token only, for the Conservative-Nationalist alliance had begun to collapse long before the
war and was now in total eclipse; the Conservatives had little to lose
in Quebec.

Inevitably the conflicts within the federal Liberal party were much
more severe. In the face of persistent rumours that a Liberal member
of the House of Commons would endorse some form of interference
in Ontario's affairs Bishop Fallon warned that any such move would

[81]*Ibid.*, Laurier to M. K. Cowan, April 11, 1916. This letter is printed in Skelton,
Laurier, II, 472–3. The phrase quoted was originally Cowan's.
[82]P.A.C., Borden Papers, OC302, T. C. Casgrain, P. E. Blondin, and E. L. Patenaude
to Borden, April 20, 1916.
[83]*Ibid.*, Borden to T. C. Casgrain, P. E. Blondin, and E. L. Patenaude, April 24, 1916.
[84]Rumilly, *Histoire*, XXI, 112.
[85]*Ibid.*, 86–8.

be "nationally dangerous" and "politically dishonest,"[86] while Rowell told Laurier that it would seriously inflame public opinion in Ontario.[87] But Laurier's reply to the latter implied that the decision to raise the question in parliament had already been taken and asserted that "if the party cannot stand up for the principles advocated, maintained and fought for by Mowat and Blake . . . it is more than time for me to step down and out."[88] In the lengthy private debate on the Mowat tradition which these comments provoked Laurier and Rowell agreed that provincial rights and justice for minorities were paramount but they were far from agreement on the current application of these principles. Rowell contended that "the minority in each province must depend upon the sense of justice and fair play of the majority to secure any redress of grievances . . . and any action . . . by the Federal Parliament would . . . be looked upon as an interference with the free action of the province in settling its own problems."[89] Laurier agreed with Rowell's belief that, in order to divert attention from the government's incompetence in handling the war effort, the Conservatives were exploiting the racial issue which they themselves had done so much to create by nourishing the Nationalist movement, yet he could not break the force of the Nationalists as long as the Ontario minority was treated unjustly and the toleration practised by Mowat was denied. Laurier rejected disallowance, but he asked, "does the idea of provincial rights go to the extent that it will not receive the complaint of a minority?"; there was ample precedent for the federal parliament if it wanted to make representations to a provincial legislature.[90] But Rowell maintained his objection to comment of any kind from the Dominion parliament: "Of course, it is the duty of any Government to consider all complaints presented to it; but complaints by residents of this province are one thing; resolutions or other proceedings by the Federal Parliament are of an entirely different character."[91] Laurier could only conclude that he and Rowell "had reached a line of cleavage . . . final and beyond redemption."[92]

[86]P.A.C., Murphy Papers, Fallon to Charles Murphy, April 14, 1916. Murphy, who was, at least by his own account, Laurier's most vigorous and faithful political manager in Ontario, had earlier boasted that he had been able, by astute behind-the-scenes organizing "to secure practically the unanimous support of the English-speaking Catholics for the Liberal party." Laurier Papers, Murphy to Laurier, June 19, 1911.

[87]Laurier Papers, Rowell to Laurier, April 15, 1916.

[88]Ibid., Laurier to Rowell, April 18, 1916.

[89]Ibid., Rowell to Laurier, April 26, 1916; see also Rowell Papers, Rowell to Laurier, May 9, 1916.

[90]Rowell Papers, Laurier to Rowell, April 28, 1916; see also Laurier to Rowell, May 11, 1916.

[91]Ibid., Rowell to Laurier, May 9, 1911.

[92]Laurier Papers, Laurier to Rowell, May 11, 1916. This letter is printed in Skelton, Laurier, II, 477.

Ernest Lapointe's resolution of May 10 in the House of Commons[93] threatened to make the rift between the Ontario Liberals and the federal leadership complete. In support of the resolution, Laurier delivered one of his last great addresses in the Commons, with its impassioned appeal not to "constitutional arguments . . . or the cold letter of any positive law . . . but to the sober reasoning and judgment of my fellow-countrymen of all origins." This alone, he felt, could persuade the people of Ontario to take a fresh look at Regulation 17 and prevent Canadians of both races from allowing the language question to poison their thinking about the nation's participation in the war.[94] In opposing the resolution Borden argued that there was no proof that Regulation 17 worked an injustice on French Canadians in Ontario and quoted the Laurier of 1896 on federal intervention in educational affairs.[95] When the vote was called five Conservatives, all from Quebec, supported the Lapointe resolution. All the Liberals from Quebec and the Maritimes voted for it, while all eleven Western Liberals opposed; most of the Ontario men were strongly disposed to vote against it too, but in the end they supported it out of personal loyalty to "the Old Man" who had indicated that he could only resign if the Ontario group went against him.[96]

While the *Globe* castigated the federal party leaders for allowing the introduction of the Lapointe resolution, Rowell, after paying tribute to the tone of Laurier's address in the House, once more denied the constitutionality and the political wisdom of the resolution; the Ontario Liberal party was convinced that just as Mowat had resisted the plea that the Ontario legislature should support an appeal for the disallowance of the Jesuit Estates Act, so the Quebec Liberals should follow the same course now that the situation was reversed. The circumstances were not precisely the same, Rowell admitted; the Lapointe resolution was not a request for disallowance, yet it was more than a personal appeal from a member or group in the House and, in principle, involved "a certain supervisory relation on the part of the Federal Government of Provincial Legislation," and it could do no good, either for relations between Ontario and Quebec, or for the minority in Ontario:

If, upon a question so vital as the province's control over her own educational

[93]Canada. *House of Commons Debates*, May 10, 1916, 3676. The resolution moved "That this House . . . while fully respecting the principle of provincial rights and the necessity of every child being given a thorough English education, respectfully suggest to the Legislative Assembly [of Ontario] the wisdom of making it clear that the privilege of the children of French parentage of being taught in their mother tongue be not interfered with."
[94]*Ibid.*, 3697–3709.
[95]*Ibid.*, 3690–6.
[96]Skelton, *Laurier*, II, 484.

affairs, the Liberal party in this province should surrender its views to the views of the party leaders at Ottawa, it would not only be doing what I believe to be wrong to the Province, but it would be committing political suicide. Surely we should not be expected to do this.[97]

Bishop Fallon was also distressed by the Lapointe resolution, and especially by the fact that the leading Irish Catholic member from Ontario, Charles Murphy, had supported Laurier and Lapointe:

> Your public approval of . . . the Lapointe resolution lends your countenance to the baseless and mischievous statement that the French Canadians are an oppressed minority in Ontario. . . . politically, educationally, and religiously, the French Canadians in Ontario have far more . . . than they can [justly] . . . claim. It seems to me that I have heard you say as much.
>
> There is, however, an aspect of your public attitude on this question which calls for the plainest rebuke. I speak as a member of another minority—the unfortunate Irish Catholics. In Quebec, in the Maritime provinces, in Ontario and throughout the whole Northwest, tens of thousands of the men and women of the race to which you and I belong have been lost to the Faith—and that is my only concern—through the callous neglect, the quiet persecution, and the continuous opposition of that same minority of which you now make yourself the champion. You need not travel beyond your own city for undoubted evidence of the truth of my statement. You will not wonder then that many of us are in amazement at the stand you have taken and ask ourselves what is to become of us between the upper millstone of French-Canadian nationalism and the lower millstone of Protestant bigotry.[98]

Faced with the strong possibility of a serious break with the Ontario Liberals, Laurier made plans to go to Toronto immediately after prorogation "in a last attempt to clear up what is becoming an intolerable situation."[99] He was armed with evidence that his understanding of the term "hitherto" in Regulation 17 was well founded—evidence in the form of copies of letters from the Department of Education to the Windsor School Board prohibiting the use of French in a new school in "a place where French has been the language of many for more than two hundred years."[100] Laurier's visit to Toronto convinced him that matters were not quite as desperate as he had supposed, although they were serious enough. If the Irish could be restrained something might be salvaged from the party's disunity in that quarter,[101] since the party as a whole did not feel as violently on the bilingual issue as his Toronto informants had led him to believe. "The resolution will have no effect in any part of the province, if our friends have the courage to maintain that it is right. This, however, will not be done in Toronto, and all the

[97]Rowell Papers, Rowell to Laurier, May 19, 1916.
[98]Murphy Papers, Fallon to Murphy, May 16, 1916.
[99]Laurier Papers, Laurier to Rowell, May 16, 1916.
[100]*Ibid.*, Laurier to Stewart Lyon, May 13, 1916.
[101]*Ibid.*, Laurier to Rodolphe Lemieux, May 26, 1916.

damage we will suffer will come from that direction,"[102] and in particular from the Toronto Liberal press.[103]

For a time, after their discussions with Laurier, Toronto Liberals ceased to make a public issue of the bilingual question. Beyond a few relatively unimpassioned assertions of Ontario's right to control her own affairs neither the *Globe* nor the *Star* had much to say on the subject for some weeks. Early in June when one hundred and fifty leading Liberals from all parts of the province met to consider party policy "there was not a solitary word on bilingual troubles."[104] An uneasy truce was maintained until the early autumn of 1916 when Laurier took exception to a *Star* editorial which had asserted that the sole purpose of Regulation 17 was to ensure that every child received an English education.[105]

This is not the policy which has again and again been put forward in the *Orange Sentinel* and in the *Toronto News*, and which is being carried out insidiously but effectively by the introduction of the word "hitherto" in the fourth paragraph of Regulation 17. No amount of quibbling by Mr. Ferguson has been able to explain this away.[106]

The editor of the *Star*, Joseph Atkinson, who was well able to speak for the inner circles of Toronto Liberalism, asserted that the total exclusion of French was not the intention of any responsible persons known to him; it was, he claimed, the extreme statements of the Orangemen which had given the French Canadians the impression that the real aim was more rigorous. Whatever the theoretical interpretation of the word "hitherto," the regulation must be judged on the basis of its enforcement; he knew of at least two schools where permission to give instruction in French had been granted since the adoption of the regulation, and he believed that the department was disposed to interpret the ruling generously.[107]

During this "era of good feeling" the first project of the Bonne Entente movement was carried out when about fifty prominent Ontario citizens visited Quebec in early October. Although participation was

[102]*Ibid.*, Laurier to W. M. German, May 27, 1916.
[103]*Ibid.*, Laurier to E. M. Macdonald, May 27, 1916.
[104]*Ibid.*, P. C. Larkin to Laurier, June 7, 1916.
[105]*Toronto Daily Star*, Sept. 15, 1916.
[106]Laurier Papers, Laurier to J. E. Atkinson, Sept. 20, 1916.
[107]*Ibid.*, Atkinson to Laurier, Sept. 20, 1916. The Deputy Minister of Education would have agreed with Atkinson's comments on his department's policy. "The French language was in no sense proscribed by it. On the contrary, what is considered a generous provision for the use of French . . . was made. . . . A number of French schools have adopted it. No complaint from them has reached the Department that in the working out of the law French is proscribed or neglected. The law has been, and will be enforced in a reasonable and considerate spirit." Dr. A. H. U. Colquhoun to Lt.-Gov. J. S. Hendrie, Feb. 17, 1916, in "Correspondence . . . concerning the Bi-lingual School Issue."

by no means confined to Liberals, they were the leading spirits in both provinces and the idea had been conceived by a correspondent of the *Toronto Star*, Arthur Hawkes, a journalist much admired by Laurier. The scheme must be understood, at least in part, as an attempt to save the Liberal party from the destruction with which it was threatened by the widening abyss between the two races created by the bilingual issue and the war,.and as a design to restore the trade position of English-speaking manufacturers in Montreal. The Ontario pilgrims to Quebec had not long returned when there occurred two events which did more to bank the fires of the language controversy than any truce among party leaders or cordial speeches at Bonne Entente dinners.[108]

The first of these was the publication of the papal encyclical, *Commisso divinitus*, the Vatican's answer to the many representations received from both Irish and French Catholics over the past six years. Pope Benedict XV deplored the enmity and rivalry which had allowed even priests to take an unseemly part in a controversy which threatened the peace and unity of the Canadian church, counselled moderation by all, and said that the bishops most directly concerned must decide on the specific questions at issue. But, the Pope cautioned:

> Let the Catholics of the Dominion remember that the one thing of supreme importance above all others is to have Catholic schools, and not to imperil their existence. . . . However, these two requirements are to be met, namely, a thorough knowledge of English and an equitable teaching of French for French-Canadian children.[109]

Although a minority of the Quebec press asserted that the Nationalist cause had been vindicated, clearly there was little reason for thinking so. This was well illustrated by the silence of Bourassa and *Le Devoir* on the encyclical and the rather vague approval given it by most of the French-speaking papers.[110] On the other hand, Bishop Fallon was pleased with the Pope's letter but anxious lest the French-Canadian bishops find it possible to place upon the call to moderation an interpretation other than his own; he therefore prepared a lengthy memorandum for a meeting of the Ontario bishops called by Cardinal Bégin to consider the apostolic letter.[111] Fallon asserted that one of the worst features of the bilingual controversy was the fact that it had undermined a great source of respect for the Roman Catholic Church—its support of lawful authority and a conservative society. The papal

[108]Rumilly, *Histoire*, XXI, 180.
[109]*Globe*, Oct. 27, 1916. The encyclical is also printed in full in Sissons, *Bilingual Schools*, Appendix 3.
[110]Rumilly, *Histoire*, XXI, 188–192.
[111]"Correspondence . . . concerning the Bi-lingual Schools," memorandum of Bishop Fallon for the bishops of Ontario, January 24, 1917.

encyclical had restored that respect, as witness the absence of a single hostile word about it in the English-Canadian press. How great then was the responsibility of the bishops to refrain from any action "that would in the public mind be judged as sympathetic with the dying agitation" which had previously done so much "to jeopardize our entire Catholic school system in Ontario." After a detailed analysis of "the preposterous demands" of the French-Canadian Education Association and its defiance of the moderate course which he had advocated for so long amid so much misunderstanding (and which was now vindicated by His Holiness), Fallon declared that "never before had the French language legally enjoyed such privileges as it does under this much-maligned Regulation 17"; previously, it had depended solely on the good faith of the government but now it had legal protection to the end of the second form.

When the Ontario episcopate met, the three French-speaking members failed to accept Fallon's interpretation of the papal letter,[112] although this fact was not evident in the pastoral letter read in all Ontario churches ten days later. The letter enjoined obedience to "the just laws and regulations enacted from time to time by the civil authorities," asserted that much of the earlier unrest was due to doubt about the meaning of the school regulations, and expressed confidence that the discretionary powers given to the Minister of Education would be used liberally.[113]

A week after the publication of the papal encyclical the waters were calmed further by the Privy Council decision in the two cases referred from the Ontario courts. Although the legislation establishing the Ottawa School Commission was ruled *ultra vires*,[114] Regulation 17 was declared *intra vires*,[115] and the government of Ontario had thus won the essential point. Although their Lordships regretted that the regulation was "couched in obscure language" so that it was "not easy to ascertain its true effect," they found that it was only denominational and not language privileges which were guaranteed under the B.N.A. Act and the Department of Education was free to make any ruling concerning the teaching of French.

While the question hung fire as to whether Quebec and the Ontario minority would accept these ecclesiastical and constitutional defeats gracefully, a Bonne Entente group from Quebec paid a return visit to Toronto and Hamilton when Hearst, Rowell, and Gouin vied with one another in supporting the war effort and national unity.[116] But Senator

112Rumilly, *Histoire*, XXII, 25.
113*Globe*, Feb. 5, 1917.
114*Ottawa Separate Schools Trustees* v. *Ottawa* [1917], A.C. 76.
115*Ottawa Separate Schools Trustees* v. *Mackell* [1917], A.C. 62.
116*Canadian Annual Review*, 1917, 476.

Landry and the members of the French-Canadian Education Association were not devotees of the Bonne Entente. The day after the reading of the pastoral letter of the Ontario bishops Landry urged a fight to the finish against Regulation 17,[117] and the Orange Order soon replied with the threat of a campaign for total abolition of separate schools if the bilingual agitation were revived.[118]

The Ontario government had still to find some way of enforcing Regulation 17, notably in Ottawa. Thus the issue reappeared in the Legislature in the winter of 1917 with the introduction of a bill to appoint another commission to take over the duties of the Ottawa Separate School Board if it persisted in its resistance. The government apparently believed that the bill was sufficiently different from the earlier measure to pass the scrutiny of the courts. Although Rowell doubted the constitutionality of the new bill, and said so publicly,[119] he and his party, except for the five French-speaking members, did not oppose it. Rowell explained this apparent inconsistency to Laurier:

> We cannot put ourselves in the position of appearing to excuse non-compliance with the law.
> Many of our members think the bill . . . is deliberately introduced with the view to laying a trap for us, and that if we opposed it they would go through all the country in their campaign trying to link us up with the opposition of the Ottawa School Board to the regulation. We cannot permit them to put us in this position.[120]

A further bill empowering the Ontario government to collect from the city of Ottawa the $300,000 spent during the time it had operated the Ottawa separate schools under the recent commission, now declared illegal, was greeted with a mild protest from Rowell on constitutional grounds, but all the English-speaking Liberals voted for it.[121] Once more Laurier was disgusted with the Ontario Liberal party.[122]

While these two bills were before the legislature the dispute between the English and French wings in the church continued, although no longer before the public gaze, and Cardinal Bégin was impelled to send two envoys to the Vatican for further advice. Thus, by midsummer of 1917, feeling over the bilingual schools was still acute among Roman Catholics, at least among the bishops, and Senator Landry talked of possible bloodshed and even of schism.[123] On the other hand, the English-speaking Protestants, being supported now by

[117]Globe, Feb. 6, 1917.
[118]Ibid., March 15, 1917.
[119]Ibid., March 31, 1917.
[120]Laurier Papers, Rowell to Laurier, March 29, 1917.
[121]Globe, April 4, 1917.
[122]Laurier Papers, Laurier to Rowell, April 4, 1917.
[123]Rumilly, Histoire, XXII, 45.

the Privy Council decision and drawing more comfort from the recent papal encyclical than the leaders of the French-Canadian Education Association, were calmer than they had been in some years. Within the two provincial parties there was only one slight breach in the wall of resistance to any alteration in Regulation 17—the five French-speaking Liberals were at odds with the rest of their party, but they were too few to be significant. The Conservatives rightly believed that the Liberals were never seriously tempted to question the basic premise of Regulation 17[124]—that English was *the* language of the province and all must learn it. The vast majority of the people of Ontario rejected entirely the concept of cultural duality.

In their private and public discussions Laurier and Rowell separated the bilingual schools issue from their disagreement over coalition with the Conservatives, which Rowell began to urge upon Laurier early in 1917, and from the conscription issue which eventually brought the two leaders to the parting of the ways. But extremists in both Ontario and Quebec made no such distinction. Bourassa and the Nationalists declared frequently that the defeat of "the Prussians of Ontario" had a prior claim over the war in Europe. On the other side, the essentially bipartisan policy of the provincial parties on the bilingual problem reinforced the traditional disposition of most Ontarians to display a united front against French Canada. The necessity of "making the French Canadians do their duty" was a prominent feature of Unionist publicity in Ontario during the conscription election of 1917. Although it is impossible to isolate this from other factors in the campaign, the emotions already aroused by the language struggle help to explain the victory of Union government candidates in all but eight of Ontario's eighty-two seats.

[124]Borden, Henry, ed., *Robert Laird Borden: His Memoirs* (2 vols., Toronto, 1938), II, 588.